THE DHAMMAPADA

As irrigators guide water to their fields,
as archers aim arrows,
as carpenters carve wood,
the wise shape their lives. (145)

Also in This Series

❂

THE BHAGAVAD GITA

THE UPANISHADS

THE
DHAMMAPADA

EKNATH EASWARAN

JAICO PUBLISHING HOUSE

Ahmedabad Bangalore Bhopal Chennai
Delhi Hyderabad Kolkata Lucknow. Mumbai

Published by Jaico Publishing House
A-2 Jash Chambers, 7-A Sir Phirozshah Mehta Road
Fort, Mumbai - 400 001
jaicopub@jaicobooks.com
www.jaicobooks.com

Published in arrangement with
Nilgiri Press
P.O. Box 256
Tomales, California 94971, USA
www.easwaran.org

THE DHAMMAPADA
ISBN 978-81-8495-092-2

First Jaico Impression: 2010
Second Jaico Impression: 2010

Printed by
Snehesh Printers
320-A, Shah & Nahar Ind. Est. A-1
Lower Parel, Mumbai - 400 013.

ᴑᴉ *Table of Contents*

FOREWORD

▯ *The Classics of Indian Spirituality*

IMAGINE A VAST hall in Anglo-Saxon England, not long after the passing of King Arthur. It is the dead of winter and a fierce snowstorm rages outside, but a great fire fills the space within the hall with warmth and light. Now and then, a sparrow darts in for refuge from the weather. It appears as if from nowhere, flits about joyfully in the light, and then disappears again, and where it comes from and where it goes next in that stormy darkness, we do not know.

Our lives are like that, suggests an old story in Bede's medieval history of England. We spend our days in the familiar world of our five senses, but what lies beyond that, if anything, we have no idea. Those sparrows are hints of something more outside – a vast world, perhaps, waiting to be explored. But most of us are happy to stay where we are. We may even be a bit afraid to venture into the unknown. What would be the point, we wonder. Why should we leave the world we know?

Yet there are always a few who are not content to spend their lives indoors. Simply knowing there is something unknown beyond their reach makes them acutely restless. They have to see what lies outside – if only, as Mallory said of Everest, "because it's there."

This is true of adventurers of every kind, but especially of those who seek to explore not mountains or jungles but consciousness itself: whose real drive, we might say, is not so much to know the unknown as to know the knower. Such men and women can be found in every age and every culture. While the rest of us stay put, they quietly slip out to see what lies beyond.

Then, so far as we can tell, they disappear. We have no idea where they have gone; we can't even imagine. But every now and then, like friends who have run off to some exotic land, they send back reports: breathless messages describing fantastic adventures, rambling letters about a world beyond ordinary experience, urgent telegrams begging us to come and see. "Look at this view! Isn't it breathtaking? Wish you could see this. Wish you were here."

The works in this set of translations – the Upanishads, the Bhagavad Gita, and the Dhammapada – are among the earliest and most universal of messages like these, sent to inform us that there is more to life than the everyday experience of our senses. The Upanishads are the oldest, so varied that we feel some unknown collectors must have tossed into a jumble all the photos, postcards, and letters from this world that they could find, without any regard for source or circumstance.

Thrown together like this, they form a kind of ecstatic slide show – snapshots of towering peaks of consciousness taken at various times by different observers and dispatched with just the barest kind of explanation. But those who have traveled those heights will recognize the views: "Oh, yes, that's Everest from the northwest – must be late spring. And here we're south, in the full snows of winter."

The Dhammapada, too, is a collection – traditionally, sayings of the Buddha, one of the very greatest of these explorers of consciousness. In this case the messages have been sorted, but not by a scheme that makes sense to us today. Instead of being grouped by theme or topic, they are gathered according to some dominant characteristic like a symbol or metaphor – flowers, birds, a river, the sky – that makes them easy to commit to memory. If the Upanishads are like slides, the Dhammapada seems more like a field guide. This is lore picked up by someone who knows every step of the way through these strange lands. He can't take us there, he explains, but he can show us the way: tell us what to look for, warn about missteps, advise us about detours, tell us what to avoid. Most important, he urges us that it is our destiny as human beings to make this journey ourselves. Everything else is secondary.

And the third of these classics, the Bhagavad Gita, gives us a map and guidebook. It gives a systematic overview of the territory, shows various approaches to the summit with their benefits and pitfalls, offers recommendations, tells us what to pack and what to leave behind. More than either of the others, it gives the sense of a personal guide. It asks and answers the questions that you or I might ask – questions not about philosophy or mysticism, but about how to live effectively in a world of challenge and change. Of these three, it is the Gita that has been my own personal guidebook, just as it was Mahatma Gandhi's.

These three texts are very personal records of a landscape that is both real and universal. Their voices, passionately human, speak directly to you and me. They describe the topography of consciousness itself, which belongs as much to us today as to these largely anonymous seers thousands of years ago. If the landscape seems dark in the light of sense perception, they tell us, it has an illumination of its own, and once our eyes adjust we can see in what Western mystics call this "divine dark" and verify their descriptions for ourselves.

And this world, they insist, is where we belong. This wider field of consciousness is our native land. We are not cabin-dwellers, born to a life cramped and confined; we are meant to explore, to seek, to push the limits of our potential as human beings. The world of the senses is just a base camp: we are meant to be as much at home in consciousness as in the world of physical reality.

This is a message that thrills men and women in every age and culture. It is for such kindred spirits that these texts were originally composed, and it is for them in our own time that

I undertook these translations, in the conviction that they deserve an audience today as much as ever. If these books speak to even a handful of such readers, they will have served their purpose.

INTRODUCTION

I: *The Dhammapada*

IF ALL OF the New Testament had been
lost, it has been said, and only the Sermon on the Mount had
managed to survive these two thousand years of history, we
would still have all that is necessary for following the teachings of Jesus the Christ. The body of Buddhist scripture is
much more voluminous than the Bible, but I would not hesi-
tate to make a similar claim: if everything else were lost, we
would need nothing more than the Dhammapada to follow
the way of the Buddha.

The Dhammapada has none of the stories, parables, and
extended instruction that characterize the main Buddhist
scriptures, the sutras. It is a collection of vivid, practical
verses, gathered probably from direct disciples who wanted
to preserve what they had heard from the Buddha himself. In
the oral tradition of the sixth century before Christ, it must
have been the equivalent of a handbook: a ready reference of
the Buddha's teachings condensed in haunting poetry and
arranged by theme – anger, greed, fear, happiness, thought.

z

Yet there is nothing piecemeal about this anthology. It is a single composition, harmonious and whole, which conveys the living presence of a teacher of genius.

Dhammapada means something like "the path of dharma" – of truth, of righteousness, of the central law that all of life is one. The Buddha did not leave a static structure of belief that we can affirm and be done with. His teaching is an ongoing path, a "way of perfection" which anyone can follow to the highest good. The Dhammapada is a map for this journey. We can start wherever we are, but as on any road, the scenery – our values, our aspirations, our understanding of life around us – changes as we make progress. These verses can be read and appreciated simply as wise philosophy; as such, they are part of the great literature of the world. But for those who would follow it to the end, the Dhammapada is a sure guide to nothing less than the highest goal life can offer: Self-realization.

THE BUDDHA'S WORLD

The Legacy

When Prince Siddhartha was born, in the middle of the sixth century B.C., Indian civilization was already ancient. Perhaps fifteen hundred years had passed since wandering Aryan tribes from Central Asia, entering the Indian subcontinent along the Indus River, had found a civilization already a thousand years old, in which what I would call the defining features of the Hindu faith – the practice of meditation and the worship of God as Shiva and the Divine Mother – seem to have already been established.

The Aryans brought with them a social order presided over by priests or brahmins, the trustees of ancient hymns, rituals, and deities related to those of other lands, especially Persia, where Aryan tribes had spread. India seems to have dealt with this new religion as it has dealt with cultural imports ever since: it absorbed the new into the old. As a result, in even the earliest of the Indian scriptures – the Rig Veda, whose oldest hymns go back at least to 1500 B.C. – we find Aryan nature-gods integrated with the loftiest conceptions of mysticism. There is no inconsistency in this integration, only a very early recognition that life's supreme reality is described in many ways. "Truth is one," says a hymn of the Rig Veda; "the wise call it by different names."

From the beginning, then, two subcurrents ran through the broad river of Vedic faith. One, followed by the vast majority of people, is the social religion of the Vedas, with brahmins in charge of preserving the ancient scriptures and presiding over a complex set of rituals. But another tradition, at least as ancient, teaches that beyond ritual and the mediation of priests, it is possible through the practice of spiritual disciplines to realize directly the divine ground of life.

This ideal is sanctioned in Vedic religion as the human being's highest vocation. The opportunity is open to anyone to wrap up social obligations and retire to an ashram in the Himalayas or in the forests flanking the Ganges to learn from an illumined teacher how to realize God. This choice is often misunderstood as world-weariness, and we know that even in those most ancient times India had ascetics who tortured their bodies in the desire to free their spirit. But this is not India's classical tradition, and the typical ashram of the times is a retreat where students would live with an illumined teacher as part of his family, leading a life of outward simplicity in order to concentrate on inner growth.

Sometimes graduates of these forest academies would go on to become teachers themselves. But it was at least as likely that they would return to society, disciplined in body and mind, to make a contribution to some secular field. Some, according to legend, became counselors of kings; one, Janaka, actually was a king. These men and women turned inward for the same reason that scientists and adventurers turn outward: not to run from life, but to master it. They went into the forests of the Ganges to find God as a poet turns to poetry or a musician to music, because they loved life so intensely that nothing would do but to grasp it at the heart. They yearned to *know*: to know what the human being is, what life is, what death means and whether it can be conquered.

Oral records of their discoveries began to be collected around 1000 B.C. or even earlier, in fragments called the Upanishads. Individualistic in their expression, yet com-

pletely universal, these ecstatic documents belong to no particular religion but to all mankind. They are not systematic
philosophy; they are not philosophy at all. Each Upanishad
contains the record of a *darshana*: literally something seen, a
view not of the world of everyday experience but of the deep,
still realms beneath the sense-world, accessible in deep meditation:

> The eye cannot see it; mind cannot grasp it.
> The deathless Self has neither caste nor race,
> Neither eyes nor ears nor hands nor feet.
> Sages say this Self is infinite in the great
> And in the small, everlasting and changeless,
> The source of life.
>
> As the web issues out of the spider
> And is withdrawn, as plants sprout from the earth,
> As hair grows from the body, even so,
> The sages say, this universe springs from
> The deathless Self, the source of life.
>   *(Mundaka* 1.1.6–7*)*

Born in freedom and stamped with the joy of Self-realization, these early testaments of the Vedic sages are clear ante-
cedents of the Buddha's voice. They contain no trace of world-
denial, no shadow of fear, no sense of diffidence about our
place in an alien universe. Far from deprecating physical existence, they teach that Self-realization means health, vitality,
long life, and a harmonious balance of inward and outward

activity. With a triumphant voice, they proclaim that human destiny lies ultimately in human hands for those who master the passions of the mind:

> We are what our deep, driving desire is.
> As our deep, driving desire is, so is our will.
> As our will is, so is our deed.
> As our deed is, so is our destiny.
> *(Brihadaranyaka* IV.4.5)

And they insist on *knowing*, not the learning of facts but the direct experience of truth: the one reality underlying life's multiplicities. This is not an intellectual achievement. Knowledge means realization. To know the truth one must make it real, must live it out in thought, word, and action. From that, everything else of value follows:

> As by knowing one piece of gold, dear one,
> We come to know all things made out of gold –
> That they differ only in name and form,
> While the stuff of which all are made is gold . . .
> So through that spiritual wisdom, dear one,
> We come to know that all of life is one.
> *(Chandogya* VI.1.5)

The method these sages followed in their pursuit of truth was called *brahmavidya*, the "supreme science," a discipline in which attention is focused intensely on the contents of consciousness. In practice this means meditation. The modern mind balks at calling meditation scientific, but in these sages' passion for truth, in their search for reality as something which is the same under all conditions and from all points of view, in their insistence on direct observation and systematic empirical method, we find the essence of the scientific spirit. It is not improper to call brahmavidya a series of experiments – on the mind, by the mind – with predictable, replicable results.

Yet, of course, the sages of the Upanishads took a different track from conventional science. They looked not at the world outside, but at human knowledge of the world outside. They sought invariants in the contents of consciousness and discarded everything impermanent as ultimately unreal, in the way that the sensations of a dream are seen to be unreal when one awakens. Their principle was *neti, neti atma:* "this is not the self; that is not the self." They peeled away personality like an onion, layer by layer, and found nothing permanent in the mass of perceptions, thoughts, emotions, drives, and memories that we call "I." Yet when everything individual was stripped away, an intense awareness remained: consciousness itself. The sages called this ultimate ground of personality *atman,* the Self.

The scientific temper of this method is a vital part of the Buddha's background. If, as Aldous Huxley observed, science is "the reduction of multiplicities to unities," no civilization has been more scientific. From the Rig Veda on, India's scriptures are steeped in the conviction of an all-pervasive order (*ritam*) in the whole of creation that is reflected in each part. In medieval Europe, it was the realization that there cannot be one set of natural laws governing earth and another set governing the heavens which led to the birth of classical physics. In a similar insight, Vedic India conceived of the natural world – not only physical phenomena but human action and thought – as uniformly governed by universal law.

This law is called *dharma* in Sanskrit, and the Buddha would make it the focus of his way of life. The word comes from *dhri*, which means to bear or to hold, and its root sense is the essence of a thing, the defining quality that "holds it together" as what it is. In its broadest application, *dharma* expresses the central law of life, that all things and events are part of an indivisible whole.

Probably no word is richer in connotations. In the sphere of human activity, dharma is behavior that is in harmony with this unity. Sometimes it is justice, righteousness, or fairness; sometimes simply duty, the obligations of religion or society. It also means being true to what is essential in the human being: nobility, honor, forgiveness, truthfulness, loyalty, compassion. An ancient saying declares that *ahimsa paramo dharma*: the essence of dharma, the highest law of life, is to do no harm to any living creature.

Like the Buddha, the sages of the Upanishads did not find the world capricious. Nothing in it happens by chance – not because events are predestined, but because 'everything is connected by cause and effect. Thoughts are included in this view, for they both cause things to happen and are aroused by things that happen. What we think has consequences for the world around us, for it conditions how we act.

All these consequences – for others, for the world, and for ourselves – are our personal responsibility. Sooner or later, because of the unity of life, they will come back to us. Someone who is always angry, to take a simple example, is bound to provoke anger from others. More subtly, a man whose factory pollutes the environment will eventually have to breathe air and drink water which he has helped to poison.

These are illustrations of what Hinduism and Buddhism call the law of karma. *Karma* means something done, whether as cause or effect. Actions in harmony with dharma bring good karma and add to health and happiness. Selfish actions, at odds with the rest of life, bring unfavorable karma and pain.

In this view, no divine agency is needed to punish or reward us; we punish and reward ourselves. This was not regarded as a tenet of religion but as a law of nature, as universal as the law of gravity. No one has stated it more clearly than St. Paul: "As you sow, so shall you reap. With whatever measure you mete out to others, with the same measure it shall be meted out to you."

For the Upanishadic sages, however, the books of karma could only be cleared within the natural world. Unpaid karmic debts and unfulfilled desires do not vanish when the physical body dies. They are forces which remain in the universe to quicken life again at the moment of conception when conditions are right for past karma to be fulfilled. We live and act, and everything we do goes into what we think at the present moment, so that at death the mind is the sum of everything we have done and everything we still desire to do. That sum of forces has karma to reap, and when the right context comes – the right parents, the right society, the right epoch – the bundle of energy that is the germ of personality is born again. We are not just limited physical creatures with a beginning in a particular year and an end after fourscore years and ten. We go back eons, and some of the contents of the deepest unconscious are the dark drives of an evolutionary heritage much older than the human race.

In this sense, the separate personality we identify ourselves with is something artificial. Einstein, speaking as a scientist, drew a similar conclusion in replying to a stranger who had asked for consolation on the death of his son:

A human being is part of the whole, called by us "Universe,"
a part limited in time and space. He experiences himself,
his thoughts and feelings, as something separated from the
rest – a kind of optical delusion of his consciousness. This
delusion is a kind of prison for us, restricting us to our
personal desires and to affection for a few persons nearest
to us. Our task must be to free ourselves from this prison
by widening our circle of compassion to embrace all living
creatures and the whole of nature in its beauty.

The sages of the Upanishads would find this an entirely acceptable way of describing both their idea of personality and the goal of life: *moksha,* freedom from the delusion of separateness; *yoga,* complete integration of consciousness; *nirvana,* the extinction of the sense of a separate ego. This state is not the extinction of personality but its fulfillment, and it is not achieved after death but in the midst of life.

In its broad outlines, the worldview I have sketched must have been familiar to the vast majority in the Buddha's audience: the kings and princes we read about in the sutras, the merchants and craftsmen and courtesans, and of course the numberless villagers who, then as now, made up most of India. Karma and rebirth were not philosophy to them but living realities. Moral order was taken for granted, and all looked to dharma as a universal standard for behavior.

These ideas form the background of the Buddha's life and became the currency of his message. Like Jesus, he came to teach the truths of life not to a few but to all who would listen, and the words he chose to express those truths were ones that everyone knew.

The Buddha's Times

The sixth century B.C. was a time of creative spiritual upheaval in most of the major civilizations of antiquity. Within a hundred years on either side we have Confu-

cius in China, Zoroaster in Persia, the pre-Socratic philosophers of ancient Greece, and the later prophets of Israel.

These were also times of cultural expansion, when centers of civilization in Europe and Asia were expanding their
spheres of influence in commerce and colonization. In the
Buddha's time at least sixteen kingdoms and republics lay
along the Ganges and against the Himalayan foothills, part
of an increasingly active trade route which ran westward
through the vast Persian empire of Cyrus the Great all the way
to the Mediterranean.

These contacts must have contributed to a burgeoning
urban life by the time the Buddha was born. The larger cities of this period, prospering from a rapidly growing middle class of merchants and craftsmen, were well planned
and show a remarkable sense of public-mindedness. "In no
other part of the ancient world," writes A. L. Basham, "were
the relations of man and man, and of man and the state, so
fair and humane. . . . India was a cheerful land, whose people,
each finding a niche in a complex and slowly evolving social
system, reached a higher level of kindliness and gentleness in
their mutual relationships than any other nation of antiquity."

These were also the centuries in which ancient India's scientific tradition began to blossom. Details are difficult to
trace, but by the first century after Christ, astronomy, arith-
metic, algebra, logic, linguistics, surgery, medicine, and a psy-

chology of personality were all well developed. The encounter between India and Greece when Alexander the Great reached the Indus river, 326 B.C., invites comparison between these two civilizations and gives us in the West a familiar benchmark. India, with its decimal system and the potent creation of zero, dominated mathematics as Greece did geometry, and in medicine and surgery both led the ancient world.

From such observations we can make some guess at the kind of education a doting ruler like the Buddha's father might have given his only son. Even in those days India had great centers of learning from which to draw tutors – one of the best known was Takshashila or Taxila, which lay at the crossroads between India and the Persian empire – and we know that the graduates of these institutions enjoyed a good reputation in neighboring lands. It is probably no coincidence that the Buddha, whose language is occasionally that of a physician, arose in a land with the world's greatest medical schools.

For most of India, of course, religion meant not the lofty concepts of the Upanishads but a web of Vedic rituals, presided over by brahmin priests and often overlaid with superstition. Yet Upanishads were still being created, and forest truth-seekers may have been even more numerous than in earlier times. They had in common the practice of some form of mental discipline (*yoga*) and some form of severe self-denial (*tapas*) as aids to releasing spiritual power. Beyond this, however, we find no more agreement than among the pre-Socratic philosophers who roamed Greece and Asia Minor at roughly the same time.

Many of these figures did not merely bypass religious orthodoxy but challenged it. We read of teachers and their disciples wandering about debating each other and teaching a perplexing disarray of views. Some of their arguments – that good and bad conduct make no difference, for fate decides everything; that transcendental knowledge is impossible; that life is entirely material – are perennial and have their adherents even today. Others seem intended to take issue with the Upanishads, or perhaps show what happens when an idea from the Upanishads is developed without being understood. The climate has been called pessimistic, even world-weary. Considering the cultural evidence, however, it seems more likely that this philosophic hotbed was one aspect of an expansive self-confidence in which old ideas were being challenged on every side.

Into this world, poised between the Vedic past and a new high-water mark of Indian culture, the Buddha was born. Like Jesus, it may be said, he came not to destroy tradition but to fulfill its meaning. And as Jesus rose out of the tradition of the prophets and yet transcends all traditions and breaks all molds, the Buddha, though he broke with the rituals and authority of the Vedas, stands squarely in the tradition of the

Upanishads. Vitality, a sublime self-confidence, an emphasis on direct experience in meditation without reference to any outside authority, and a passionate trust in truth, in the oneness of life, and in our human capacity to take our destiny into our own hands – all these are the very spirit of the Upanishads, and no one embodies it better than the Buddha.

Yet the Buddha brings to this spirit a genius all his own. The sages of the Upanishads sought to know, and their testaments sing with the joy of Self-realization. The Buddha sought to save, and the joy in his message is the joy of knowing that he has found a way for everyone, not just great sages, to put an end to sorrow. Meditation, once the sublime art of a very few, he offers to teach to all – not for some otherworldly goal, but as a way to happiness, health, and fulfillment in selfless service. He argues with no one, denies no faith, convinces only with truth and love. He brought not so much a new religion as *sanatana dharma,* "the eternal dharma," the name India has always given to religion itself. Like an adventurer who pawns everything to discover some priceless jewel, he sought out India's spiritual treasure and then gave it away to everyone who would take it, rich or poor, high caste or low, with a free hand; and for that reason he is loved today, twenty-five hundred years later, by perhaps one quarter of the earth's people.

LIFE & TEACHING

The early Buddhists were not biographers or historians, any more than the early Christians were. Their first passion, when their teacher was no longer with them in the body, was to record not what they knew of his past but what he had taught. Of the Buddha's life before illumination, therefore, the scriptures record only isolated fragments. From these has been pieced together the story of the Buddha as it is told today. The inconsistencies in the sources need not trouble us. Whatever their value as historical evidence, there can be no doubt that the story captures a real and deeply appealing personality.

Siddhartha Gautama was born around 563 B.C., the son of a king called Shuddhodana who ruled the lands of the Shakya clan at the foot of the Himalayas, along what is today the border between India and Nepal. Though not monarch of an empire like the neighboring kings of Kosala and Maghada, Shuddhodana was well-to-do, and his capital, Kapilavastu, had prospered from its location near the trade routes into the Ganges valley. Apparently his power was not absolute, but shared with a voting assembly called the *sangha* – the same name the Buddha would later give to his monastic order, one of the earliest democratic institutions in the world.

When the child was born, a holy man prophesied that he would either become an emperor or renounce the world for a great spiritual destiny. His parents gave him the name Siddhartha, "he whose purpose in life has been attained." Like most loving fathers, however, King Shuddhodana had little interest in seeing his son and sole heir wander off into the forest in search of truth. He ordered his ministers not to expose the boy to tragedy or allow him to lack anything he desired.

Siddhartha was an extraordinarily gifted child, and we are told that he received the best education for kingship that the world of his day could offer. He excelled in sports and physical exploits combining strength with skill – particularly archery, in which he stood out among a people famous for their prowess with the bow. He had a quick, clear intellect matched by an exquisite tenderness, a rare combination which would stamp his later life. He showed both when as a youth he saw a bird shot down by the arrow of his cousin Devadatta. Siddhartha, already dimly aware of his bond to all living creatures, tenderly removed the arrow, then took the bird home and nursed it back to health. Devadatta, furious, insisted that the bird was his, and took his case to the king. "*I* shot that bird," he said. "It's mine." But Siddhartha asked, "To whom should any creature belong: to him who tries to kill it, or to him who saves its life?"

At the age of seven or eight the prince went to the annual plowing festival, where his father ceremonially guided the bullocks in plowing the first furrow. It was a long, stressful day, and when the boy grew sleepy his family set him down to rest on a platform under a rose apple tree. When they returned, hours later, they found him seated upright in the same position as they had left him. Disturbed by the ceaseless toil of the bullocks and plowmen and the plight of the tiny creatures who lost their homes and lives in the plowing, Siddhartha had become absorbed in reflection on the transience of life. In this profound absorption he forgot himself and his surroundings completely, and a joy he had never known suffused his consciousness.

Siddhartha grew up accustomed to luxury and ease. Later he would tell the austere monks gathered around him, "I was delicately nurtured, brothers. When a piece of silk was not the very softest grade, I would not wear it next to my skin. Only the freshest fruits were sent to me, and a whole staff of cooks looked after my meals." Nothing unpleasant was allowed to enter his vision.

On attaining manhood, Siddhartha learned that a lovely cousin named Yashodhara would choose her husband from the princes and chieftains who vied for her hand in a contest of archery. Siddhartha showed up on the appointed day, supremely confident of his skill. One of the suitors hit the bull's-eye, but Siddhartha stepped forward boldly and with one shot split his rival's arrow down the middle.

Yashodhara proved to be as loving as she was lovely, and in time the couple had a son named Rahula who combined the beauty and tender nature of them both. Siddhartha was twenty-nine. His future promised every fulfillment life could offer.

By this time, however, gnawing questions had begun to haunt his mind. The innocent pleasures of his life seemed fragile, edged with the poignancy of something not quite real enough to hold on to. An awareness preoccupied him which most thoughtful people taste but seldom face: that life passes swiftly and leaves very little behind.

His questions must have been old when history began; we ask them still. Has life a purpose, or is it only a passing show? Is there nothing more to hope for than a few good friends, a loving family, some memories to savor before one goes? It was questions like these that sent many into the forests along the Ganges to the sages of the Upanishads, and Yashodhara, seeing the look in her husband's eyes, grew troubled. Even their newborn son had not brought him peace.

Finally, desperate to ease his tormented mind, Siddhartha persuaded his father to agree to a day outside the walls of his estates. Recalling the prophesy at his son's birth, King Shuddhodana made sure the city was ready. No one poor, no one sick, no one unhappy was to be present along the prince's designated route.

Yet despite all precautions, among the cheerful, cheering crowd who turned out to greet him, Siddhartha happened to catch sight of a man whose face was sallow and drawn and whose eyes were glazed with fever. "What is the matter with this man, Channa?" he asked his charioteer in horror.

"That is disease," Channa replied. "All are subject to it. If a man is mortal, disease can strike him, even if he be rich or royal."

Siddhartha continued on his excursion, but he could not forget the pallor of the man's face or the haunted look in his eyes.

The next day Siddhartha ventured outside the city again. This time he saw a bent, wrinkled woman faltering on her staff. Siddhartha regarded her with compassion. "Is this, too, disease?" he asked.

"No," Channa replied. "It is only age, which overtakes us all."

"Will my wife become like that?"

"Yes, my lord. Even Princess Yashodhara, beautiful as a full moon in a cloudless sky. One day her skin too will be wrinkled and her eyes dim, and she will falter in her steps."

"Channa, I have seen enough. Take me back!"

But in the palace Siddhartha found no peace. Before long he ventured out a third time, and on this occasion he saw a corpse stretched out on a bier for cremation. "What is that, Channa, which resembles a man but looks more like a log?"

"That was once a man, but death has come to claim him; only his body remains. Death will come for all of us, rich or poor, well or ill, young as well as old."

"Even for my newborn son?"

"Yes, my lord. He too will lie like that one day."

The prince closed his eyes and covered his ears. But a bomb had burst in the depths of his consciousness, and everything around him seemed edged with mortality.

On his way home a fourth sight arrested him: a man seated by the roadside with closed eyes, his body upright and still. "Channa, what kind of man is that? Is he dead too?"

"No. That is a *bhikshu*, who has left worldly life to seek what lies beyond. When the body seems dead but the spirit is awake, that is what they call yoga."

Siddhartha rode home deep in thought.

The rest of that day he found no peace. The roses in his garden, whose beauty had always caught his eye, now reminded him only of the evanescence of life. The bright scenes and laughter of the palace flowed by like running water. "Everything is change," he thought; "each moment comes and goes. Is there nothing more, nothing to the future but decline and death?" These questions are familiar from the lives of saints and seekers in every tradition, and there is nothing morbid about them; it is this awareness of death that brings life into clear focus. The Buddha-to-be was beginning to wake up.

Shuddhodana noticed with alarm the change that had come over his son. Gone was the enjoyment he had always found in his sports and games and the company of his friends; his mood was sober and indrawn. The king consulted with his ministers and concluded that Siddhartha had grown weary of married life and needed diversion. That very night they arranged a spectacle featuring the loveliest dancing girls in the land.

The performance went on past midnight. Finally the last guest left and the dancers fell asleep. One by one the lights burned out. Only Siddhartha remained awake, scarcely aware of the world, brooding over a still unconscious choice.

Sometime in the early hours of the morning – it was, the chronicles tell us, the first full moon of spring – Siddhartha looked around him in the shadowy hall and saw a chilling sight. The dancers lay snoring in the postures in which they had fallen asleep, and in the moonlight the lithe bodies that had seemed so lovely in silk and makeup looked coarse and offensive in their disarray. The chroniclers say it was a conjuring trick of the gods, who wanted the prince to reject the pleasures of the world and seek enlightenment. But no such explanation seems necessary. For a moment the curtain of time had gone up, and Siddhartha had seen beneath the tinsel of appearance, past the strange illusion that makes us believe the beauty of the moment can never fade.

That moment he resolved to go forth from the life he had known, not to see his family again until he had found a way to go beyond age and death. For a long moment he lingered at the doorway to his bedchamber, watching his wife and son asleep in each other's arms. Young, delicate, full of tenderness, they seemed now to stand for all creatures, so vulnerable in the face of time and change. Afraid his resolve might fail, he did not wake them.

In the dark hours before dawn Channa brought the white horse Kanthaka, his hooves padded so that no one would hear his steps in the courtyard. They traveled eastward until dawn. At the river Anoma the prince dismounted, slipped the rings and ornaments of royalty from his body, and removed his robes and sandals. "Take these back to the palace now, Channa. I must go on alone."

Channa received the bundle with tears in his eyes, for he had served the prince many years and loved him deeply. He pleaded to be allowed to go along, but to no avail. Kanthaka too, according to the chronicles, wept as Channa led him home, and died soon afterward of a broken heart.

At the edge of the forest, Siddhartha scavenged some rags from the graves of executed convicts. They too had severed their bonds with the world, and were not all creatures under sentence of death? Their color, saffron yellow, has been ever since the emblem of a Buddhist monk.

Siddhartha put on his makeshift robe, burned the rest of his clothes, and cut off his black hair. Henceforth he would own no more than his robe and a mendicant's bowl, and eat only such food as he might be given. He was ready to plunge into his quest.

In the forest, Siddhartha studied yoga – meditation – with

the best teachers he could find. With each he learned quickly
what they had to teach, mastering their disciplines and match-
ing their austerities, and discovered that they had not found
the goal he sought.

Siddhartha then struck off on his own. For six years he wan-
dered in the forest, subjecting his body to all kinds of morti-
fication. Perhaps, he reasoned, his teachers had not been austere enough to reach the goal. Perhaps through starvation he
could break his identification with his body, winning detachment from its ultimate fate.

Day by day he reduced his intake of food until he was eating only one grain of rice a day. His body became so emaci-
ated that he could reach into the cavern of his stomach and
feel his spine. Such power of will attracted attention from
other seekers, and on the banks of the river Neranjara he was
joined by five ascetics who became his disciples.

With his body so worn down, however, Siddhartha discovered that he could no longer meditate well. His mind lacked
the vitality for intense, sustained concentration. He began
casting about for another approach, and there came to his
mind the experience under the rose apple tree so long ago,
where he had tasted the joy that comes when the clamor of
the mind and senses is stilled. "Austerity is not the way to the
calming of passion, to perfect knowledge, to freedom," he
thought. "The right way is that which I practiced at the foot of

the rose apple tree. But that is not possible for someone who has spent his strength."

At that time, Sujata, the lovely daughter of a nearby house-holder, had just borne her first child and wanted to make a thanksgiving offering. "The radiant god to whom you prayed for a son," her handmaid reported, "is sitting under a banyan tree by the side of the river. Why not make your offering to him directly?" So Sujata prepared her favorite delicacies and brought them in a golden bowl to the banks of the Neranjara, where she offered them to the man whose frail frame seemed suffused with light.

Siddhartha ate slowly, and when his hunger was satisfied he twisted a wick from the ragged edge of his robe, placed it in oil in the bowl, lighted it, and set his makeshift lamp afloat in the river's slow waters. "If I am not to attain complete freedom," he declared, "let this bowl travel with the current downstream." It drifted in the eddies, then seemed to move slowly against the flow.

Siddhartha's disciples witnessed these peculiar developments with amazement. Was this the man who for six years had outdone all other seekers in austerity? They had put their trust in his unbreakable determination; when they saw him waver and change course, they abandoned him in disgust. Siddhartha was again alone.

It was spring, when the world itself was quickening with

new life. The very landscape must have reminded him of that ploughing festival so many years before, when his mind had spontaneously plunged into meditation. "When a good archer first hits the bull's-eye," he told his disciples later, "he stops and examines everything carefully. How was he standing? How was he holding the bow? How did his fingers let the arrow go? And he tries to make everything the same for the next shot. In the same way, brothers, I set about systematically trying to repeat what had led to success so long ago."

Near the city of Gaya he found a tranquil spot under a sacred fig tree and carpeted a place with fresh, fragrant grass. Folding his legs beneath him, he drew himself straight for meditation and took a solemn vow: "Come what may – let my body rot, let my bones be reduced to ashes – I will not get up from here until I have found the way beyond decay and death." It was dusk and the moon was rising, the first full moon of the first month of spring.

Thus determined, full of peace, Siddhartha passed into deep meditation, when the senses close down and concentration flows undisturbed by awareness of the outside world. Then, the chronicles say, Mara the tempter came, much as Satan came to tempt Jesus in the desert. Mara is Death and every selfish passion that ties us to a mortal body. He is "the striker," who attacks without warning and never plays by the rules. Any kind of entrapment is fair.

First Mara sent his daughters, maidens of unearthly beauty,

each accompanied by exquisite ladies-in-waiting. Any of them, Mara promised, Siddhartha could have as his own. The Buddha-to-be sat unmoved and deepened his concentration.

Next Mara assailed his meditation with fierce armies – lust, cowardice, doubt, hypocrisy, the desire for honor and fame. Like a mountain unshaken by an earthquake, Siddhartha continued his plunge into deeper consciousness.

Finally, as he neared the frontier in consciousness that divides what is transient from what is deathless, Mara appeared and challenged him in person. Who had given him the right to escape his realm?

The Buddha did not try to argue, but it is said that he placed his palm on the earth and the earth itself gave witness. The voices of millions of creatures could be heard crying out that he had come to rescue them from sorrow.

At this Mara ordered his armies to retreat. The dark waters of the unconscious closed over Siddhartha, and he slipped into that profound stillness in which thought stops and the distinctions of a separate personality dissolve. In this profound state he remained immersed throughout the night.

When dawn came the tree under which he sat burst into bloom, and a fragrant spring breeze showered him with blossoms. He was no longer Siddhartha, the finite personality that had been born in Kapilavastu. He was the Buddha, "he who is awake." He had found the way to that realm of being which decay and death can never touch: nirvana.

Unaware of his body, plunged deep in a sea of joy and free to remain there until the end of time, the Buddha could have had only a faint recollection of those still caught in selfishness and sorrow. But the needs of the world cried out to him, the chronicles say, "and his heart was moved to pity." That slim thread of recollection was enough. Drawn by the will to lead others to the freedom he had found, the Buddha traced his way back.

Then Mara played his last trump. "You have awakened to nirvana," he whispered, "and thus escaped from my realm. You have plumbed the depths of consciousness and known a joy not given even to the gods. But you know well how difficult it has been. You sought nirvana with your eyes clear, and found it almost impossible to achieve; others' eyes are covered with dust from the beginning, and they seek only their own satisfaction. Even in the midst of sorrow, do you see anyone throw the toys of the world away? If you try to teach them what you have found, who do you think will listen? Who will strive as you have? How many will even try to wipe the dust from their eyes?"

For a long time the Buddha sat silent, contemplating the impossibility of his mission. These questions shook him to the depths. In a world of sleepwalkers, how many would listen to someone returning from a world they would probably never see, coming to say that love always begets love and violence only breeds more violence? In a world guided by passions, how many would be willing to make the sacrifices required to base their lives on these truths?

Slowly his confidence returned. "Perhaps," he replied, "there will be a few who will listen. Dust does cover the eyes of all, but for some it is only a thin film. Everyone desires an end to suffering and sorrow. To those who will listen, I will teach the dharma, and for those who follow it, the dharma itself will set them free."

The Buddha remained at that spot for weeks, immersing himself in nirvana over and over. Each time he probed deep into the heart of life, the nature of happiness, and the origins of sorrow.

Then, with his teaching worked out, he went forth to teach. He had not only attained nirvana, he was established in it – aware of life's unity not only during meditation but at every moment, awake or asleep. Now he could help others to make the same crossing. A kind of cosmic ferryman, he is represented as always calling, "*Koi paraga?*Anyone for the other shore?"

The Wheel of Dharma

The Buddha's return is a pivotal moment, one of those rare events when the divine penetrates history and transfigures it. Like Moses returning from Mt. Sinai, like Jesus appearing in the crowd at the river Jordan to be baptized by John, a man who has left the world returns to serve it, no

longer merely human but charged with transcendent power.
As the scriptures record of Moses and Jesus, we can imagine
how the Buddha must have shone that bright spring morning in the Himalayan foothills. Dazzled by the radiance of his
personality, it is said, people gathered about him and asked,
"Are you a god?"

"No."

"Are you an angel?"

"No."

"What are you then?"

The Buddha smiled and answered simply, "I am awake"
– the literal meaning of the word *buddha*, from the Sanskrit
root *budh*, to wake up.

His five former disciples caught sight of him from a distance and resolved neither to shun him nor to give him special
attention. But as he drew closer, his face shining with what he
had seen and understood, they found themselves preparing a
place for him and sitting at his feet.

"Well," one of them might have asked, "did the bowl flow
upstream or down?"

"It flowed upstream, brothers," the Blessed One replied. "I
have done what is to be done. I have seen the builder of this
house" – indicating his body, but signifying his old self – "and
I have shattered its ridgepole and its rafters; that house shall
not be built again. I have found the deathless, the uncondi-

tioned; I have seen life as it is. I have entered nirvana, beyond
the reach of sorrow."

"Teach us what you have found."

Thus to these five, his first students, the Buddha began his
work of teaching the dharma, the path that leads to the end of
sorrow. The place was the Deer Park near the holy city of Varanasi on the Ganges, and the event is revered as the moment
when the Compassionate One "set in motion the wheel of the
dharma," which will never cease revolving so long as there are
men and women who follow his path.

In this talk we see the Buddha as physician to the world, the
relentlessly clear-seeing healer whose love embraces all creatures. In the Four Noble Truths, he gives his clinical observations on the human condition, then his diagnosis, then the
prognosis, and finally the cure.

"The First Truth, brothers, is the fact of suffering. All desire
happiness, *sukha*: what is good, pleasant, right, permanent,
joyful, harmonious, satisfying, at ease. Yet all find that life
brings *duhkha*, just the opposite: frustration, dissatisfaction,
incompleteness, suffering, sorrow. Life is change, and change
can never satisfy desire. Therefore everything that changes
brings suffering.

"The Second Truth is the cause of suffering. It is not life that
brings sorrow, but the demands we make on life. The cause
of duhkha is selfish desire: *trishna*, the thirst to have what

one wants and to get one's own way. Thinking life can make them happy by bringing what they want, people run after the satisfaction of their desires. But they get only unhappiness, because selfishness can only bring sorrow.

"There is no fire like selfish desire, brothers. Not a hundred years of experience can extinguish it, for the more you feed it, the more it burns. It demands what experience cannot give: permanent pleasure unmixed with anything unpleasant. But there is no end to such desires; that is the nature of the mind. Suffering because life cannot satisfy selfish desire is like suffering because a banana tree will not bear mangoes.

"There is a Third Truth, brothers. Any ailment that can be understood can be cured, and suffering that has a cause has also an end. When the fires of selfishness have been extinguished, when the mind is free of selfish desire, what remains is the state of wakefulness, of peace, of joy, of perfect health, called *nirvana*.

"The Fourth Truth, brothers, is that selfishness can be extinguished by following an eightfold path: right understanding, right purpose, right speech, right conduct, right occupation, right effort, right attention, and right meditation. If dharma is a wheel, these eight are its spokes.

"Right understanding is seeing life as it is. In the midst of change, where is there a place to stand firm? Where is there anything to have and hold? To know that happiness cannot come from anything outside, and that all things that come into being have to pass away: this is right understanding, the beginning of wisdom.

"Right purpose follows from right understanding. It means willing, desiring, and thinking that is in line with life as it is. As a flood sweeps away a slumbering village, death sweeps away those who are unprepared. Remembering this, order your life around learning to live: that is right purpose.

"Right speech, right action, and right occupation follow from right purpose. They mean living in harmony with the unity of life: speaking kindly, acting kindly, living not just for oneself but for the welfare of all. Do not earn your livelihood at the expense of life or connive at or support those who do harm to other creatures, such as butchers, soldiers, and makers of poison and weapons. All creatures love life; all creatures fear pain. Therefore treat all creatures as yourself, for the dharma of a human being is not to harm but to help.

"The last three steps, brothers, deal with the mind. Everything depends on mind. Our life is shaped by our mind; we become what we think. Suffering follows an evil thought as the wheels of a cart follow the oxen that draw it. Joy follows a pure thought like a shadow that never leaves.

"Right effort is the constant endeavor to train oneself in thought, word, and action. As a gymnast trains the body, those who desire nirvana must train the mind. Hard it is to attain nirvana, beyond the reach even of the gods. Only through ceaseless effort can you reach the goal. Earnest among the indolent, vigilant among those who slumber, advance like a race horse, breaking free from those who follow the way of the world.

"Right attention follows from right effort. It means keeping the mind where it should be. The wise train the mind to give complete attention to one thing at a time, here and now. Those who follow me must be always mindful, their thoughts focused on the dharma day and night. Whatever is positive, what benefits others, what conduces to kindness or peace of mind, those states of mind lead to progress; give them full attention. Whatever is negative, whatever is self-centered, what feeds malicious thoughts or stirs up the mind, those states of mind draw one downward; turn your attention away.

"Hard it is to train the mind, which goes where it likes and does what it wants. An unruly mind suffers and causes suffering whatever it does. But a well-trained mind brings health and happiness.

"Right meditation is the means of training the mind. As rain seeps through an ill-thatched hut, selfish passion will seep through an untrained mind. Train your mind through meditation. Selfish passions will not enter, and your mind will grow calm and kind.

"This, brothers, is the path that I myself have followed. No other path so purifies the mind. Follow this path and conquer

Mara; its end is the end of sorrow. But all the effort must be made by you. Buddhas only show the way."

The Years of Teaching

From Varanasi the Buddha set out to teach the dharma, walking through the villages and cities of north India. His fame spread before him, drawing crowds wherever he stopped, and from each place he took away with him several ardent young disciples in saffron robes and left behind a great many more who, though they could not abandon their homes and families, had consecrated themselves to the dharma. Only during the monsoon season did the Buddha not travel, taking advantage of the heavy rains to rest with his followers in a forest retreat and teach those who lived in the cities and villages nearby.

In this way he completed the second forty years of his life, and many beautiful stories are told of him during these years of wandering. A few of these will give some idea of the way he taught, and why he so swiftly captured the hearts of the Indian people.

The Homecoming

From the day Channa returned to the palace at Kapilavastu with his master's cast-off finery, the Buddha's family had mourned. Yashodhara wept for two: little Rahula, newly born the night that Siddhartha left, grew up knowing nothing of his father except what he heard from the loving accounts of those who missed him.

According to ancient Indian custom, those who renounce the world die to their past and become a new person altogether, never to go home again. Of Siddhartha's life in the forest, little more than rumor could have reached his family's ears. For seven years Yashodhara mourned without hope, while the infant that Siddhartha had left in her arms grew straight and tall.

One day Yashodhara's maids came running with the news that a buddha, an awakened one, was coming to Kapilavastu with a great following of men all in saffron robes. He taught about dharma, they said, as no one had ever taught before, with an open hand and an open heart, and it was said that he was none other than the man who had been Siddhartha.

King Shuddhodana listened to this news with joy followed by anger, for he loved his son passionately and had never forgiven him for abandoning his royal heritage. That same day he rode out into the forest where the Buddha and his disciples were staying, and demanded to see his son.

Even in those days it was Indian custom for children to greet their father by kneeling and touching his feet. Yet King Shuddhodana, unprepared for the radiance of the man who came to greet him, found himself kneeling at the feet of his son. But then seven years of frustration burst forth. Why had he left those who loved him – his father and foster mother, his wife and little son? They had given him every comfort; if he wanted something more, did he have to break their hearts to get it? And the crown of a king – did it mean so little to him that he had to go and throw it away, leaving his father alone?

The Buddha listened patiently, and even while Shuddhodana scolded, the pain in his heart began to subside. At last, abashed before this man he could no longer claim as his son, he fell silent.

Then the Buddha spoke. "Father, which is the greater ruler: he who rules a small kingdom through power, or he who rules the whole world through love? Your son, who renounced a crown, has conquered all, for he has conquered an enemy to whom all bow. You wished for a son to give you security in your old age, but what son can guarantee security from changes of fortune, from illness, from age itself, from death? I have brought you instead a treasure no other can offer: the dharma, an island in an uncertain world, a lamp in darkness, a sure path to a realm beyond sorrow."

Shuddhodana listened to these words, and the burden of sorrow slipped from his shoulders. He returned to his palace with his mind calm and clear, thinking of the treasure his son had mentioned and wondering what it would mean to accept it.

The next morning Yashodhara awoke to the sound of tumult in the streets below. Her handmaids ran to the balcony. It had not been long since the Buddha's illumination, but even if we discount the enthusiasm of tradition he had already gathered a large following, and that regal figure at the head of a stream of bright saffron must have made a splendid sight. "How like a god he looks!" her maidens called. "Mistress, come and see!"

Yashodhara did not join them, but called Rahula to her side. "Do you see that radiant figure," she said, "who owns only a mendicant's bowl and robe, yet carries himself like a king? That is your father. Run down and ask him for your inheritance."

Rahula disappeared down the stairs, and the women watched him reappear in the courtyard below and push his way through the crowd until he stood squarely in front of the man in saffron waiting at the palace gate. The boy fell at his father's feet and boldly repeated his mother's words. Yashodhara's handmaids could not have heard the exchange, but they saw the Buddha lift Rahula to his feet with a sweet smile, and remove the gold-hemmed wearing cloth from the boy's shoulder to replace it with one of saffron. Rahula, seven, had become the first and only child permitted to join the Buddha's disciples.

"Mistress," Yashodhara's maids pleaded, "you must go down to him too! There, the king himself has gone to greet him. Surely he will see you, even if he is a monk and it is against his vows to look on a woman."

"No," said Yashodhara. "If there is any worth in my love, he will come to me."

The maids protested, but through their talk came shocked cries from the crowd below and then the sound of footsteps on the stairs. The door opened on King Shuddhodana, and behind him stood the Buddha himself. As he crossed the threshold to her chambers Yashodhara knelt in his path, clasped his ankles, and laid her head on his feet.

"Since the day you left," Shuddhodana said, "she has mourned, but she has followed your way. When Channa brought back your robes and jewelry, she put aside her finery. You slept on the forest floor, so she gave up her bed for a mat. When she heard you were eating only once a day, she too resolved to eat only once a day."

The Buddha stooped down and raised her to her feet. "You have not yet heard a word of the dharma," he said, "but in your love you have followed me without question for many lives. The time for tears is over. I will teach you the way that leads beyond sorrow, and the love you have shown to me will embrace the entire world."

The Order of Women

While the Buddha was in Kapilavastu many in his family, even his father, came to seek permission to join the monastic order he had established for his male followers. There were no women in the Order, however, and although those dearest to his heart – Yashodhara and his aunt and foster mother, Prajapati – earnestly sought to join, the Buddha refused to make the precedent. Asking men and women to live together in a homeless life while trying to master the natural human passions seemed too much to expect of human nature. For women, his recommendation was the same as for men who wanted to follow him but were not prepared to give up home and family. There is no need to take to the monastic life, he told them, in order to follow dharma. All the disciplines of the Eightfold Path, including meditation, can be followed by householders if they do their best to give up selfish attachment.

Yet this was not enough for Yashodhara and Prajapati. They had seen through the superficial satisfactions of life and longed to dedicate themselves completely to its goal. After the Buddha left Kapilavastu they decided to go after him on foot, like pilgrims, to press their case.

They caught up with him at Vaishali, almost two hundred miles away. Ananda, a young disciple who loved the Buddha passionately and attended to all his personal needs, happened to see them first, and his heart immediately understood their devotion and moved him to take their side. But the Buddha had already made his decision, and Ananda could not think of any way to bring the subject up again. He came to his teacher that afternoon troubled and preoccupied, not knowing what to say.

"What is it, Ananda? There is a cloud over your face today."

"Blessed One," Ananda said, "my mind keeps struggling with a question I cannot answer. Is it only men who are capable of overcoming suffering?"

The Buddha never answered idle questions, but Ananda was very dear to him, and clearly there was something on his mind. "No, Ananda," he replied. "Every human being has the capacity to overcome suffering."

"Is it only men who are capable of renouncing selfish attachments for the sake of attaining nirvana?"

"No, Ananda. It is rare, but every human being has the capacity to renounce worldly attachments for the sake of attaining nirvana."

"Blessed One, if that is true, should only men be allowed to join the *sangha* and devote themselves completely to the Way?"

The Buddha must have smiled, for Ananda had caught him with both love and logic. "No, Ananda. If someone longs as ardently as I have to give up everything and follow the Way, then man or woman, it would be wrong to block that person's path. Everyone must be free to attain the goal."

Ananda's eyes shone with gratitude. He got up and opened the door, and there stood the two barefooted women waiting for their reply.

"Ananda," the Buddha laughed, "by all this, you have said and done just as I would have said and done."

Thus were ordained the first nuns of the Buddha's order, and the two branches of the sangha became the world's first monastic community.

The Middle Path

The Buddha's students came from many different backgrounds. Ananda and Devadatta, his cousins, left behind wealth and social position; Shariputra, Maudgalyayana, and Kashyapa were ascetics won over to the Buddha's path. Upali had been a barber in Kapilavastu. And Sona, also from a wealthy family, had entertained hopes of being a musician, for he loved to play the *vina*.

When Sona took to the spiritual life, he did so with such zeal that he decided everything else must be thrown overboard. Despite wild animals and poisonous snakes, he went off into the forest alone to practice meditation – and to undo the softness of his pampered past, he insisted on going barefoot.

After some time of this the Buddha decided to go after him. The path was not hard to find, for it was stained with blood from Sona's feet. In addition to his begging bowl, the Blessed One brought something unusual: a vina, whose strings he had loosened until they were as limp as spaghetti.

He found Sona meditating under a banyan tree. The boy limped over to greet him, but the Buddha did not seem to notice. All he said was, "Sona, can you show me how to make music with this?"

Sona took the instrument respectfully and fingered a few notes. Then he began to laugh. "Blessed One," he said, "you can't produce music when the strings are so loose!"

"Oh, I see. Let me try again." And he proceeded to wind the strings so tightly that Sona winced. When the Buddha tested them, all that came out was high-pitched squeaks.

"Blessed One, that won't work either. You'll break the strings. Here, let me tune it for you." He took the instrument, loosened the strings gently, and played a little of a haunting song.

Then he stopped, for the music brought memories he was afraid to awaken. "It has to be tuned just right to make music," he said abruptly, handing the vina back to the Buddha. "Neither too tight nor too loose. Just right."

"Sona," the Buddha replied, "it is the same for those who seek nirvana. Don't let yourself be slack, but don't stretch yourself to breaking either. The middle course, lying between too much and too little, is the way of my Eightfold Path."

Malunkyaputra
The Buddha's penetrating insight attracted many intellectuals, one of whom, Malunkyaputra, grew more and more frustrated as the Buddha failed to settle certain basic metaphysi-

cal questions. Finally he went to the Buddha in exasperation and confronted him with the following list:

"Blessed One, there are theories which you have left unexplained and set aside unanswered: Whether the world is eternal or not eternal; whether it is finite or infinite; whether the soul and body are the same or different; whether a person who has attained nirvana exists after death or does not, or whether perhaps he both exists and does not exist, or neither exists nor does not. The fact that the Blessed One has not explained these matters neither pleases me nor suits me. If the Blessed One will not explain this to me, I will give up spiritual disciplines and return to the life of a layman."

"Malunkyaputra," the Buddha replied gently, "when you took to the spiritual life, did I ever promise you I would answer these questions?"

Malunkyaputra was probably already sorry for his outburst, but it was too late. "No, Blessed One, you never did."

"Why do you think that is?"

"Blessed One, I haven't the slightest idea!"

"Suppose, Malunkyaputra, that a man has been wounded by a poisoned arrow, and his friends and family are about to call a doctor. "Wait!" he says. "I will not let this arrow be removed until I have learned the caste of the man who shot me. I have to know how tall he is, what family he comes from, where they live, what kind of wood his bow is made from, what fletcher made his arrows. When I know these things, you can proceed to take the arrow out and give me an anti-dote for its poison." What would you think of such a man?"

"He would be a fool, Blessed One," replied Malunkyaputra shamefacedly. "His questions have nothing to do with getting the arrow out, and he would die before they were answered."

"Similarly, Malunkyaputra, I do not teach whether the world is eternal or not eternal; whether it is finite or infinite; whether the soul and the body are the same or different; whether a person who has attained nirvana exists after death or does not, or whether perhaps he both exists and does not exist, or neither exists nor does not. I teach how to remove the arrow: the truth of suffering, its origin, its end, and the Noble Eightfold Path."

Teaching With an Open Hand

"Perhaps," a disciple suggested discreetly on another occasion, "these are matters which the Blessed One himself has not cared to know."

The Buddha did not answer, but smiled and took a handful of leaves from the branch of the tree under which they sat. "What do you think," he asked, "are there more leaves in my hand or on this tree?"

"Blessed One, you know your handful is only a small part of what remains on the branches. Who can count the leaves of a shimshapa tree?"

"What I know," the Buddha said, "is like the leaves on that

tree; what I teach is only a small part. But I offer it to all with an open hand. What do I not teach? Whatever is fascinating to discuss, divides people against each other, but has no bearing on putting an end to sorrow. What do I teach? Only what is necessary to take you to the other shore."

The Handful of Mustard Seed

Once, near the town of Shravasti, the Buddha was seated with his disciples when a woman named Krisha Gautami made her way through the crowd and knelt at his feet. Her tear-streaked face was wild with grief, and in the fold of her sari she carried a tiny child.

"I've been to everyone," she pleaded desperately, "but still my son will not move, will not breathe. Can't you save him? Can't the Blessed One work miracles?"

"I can help you, sister," the Buddha promised tenderly. "But first I will need a little mustard seed – and it must come from a house where no one has died."

Giddy with joy, Krisha Gautami raced back to the village and stopped at the very first house. The woman who met her was full of understanding. "Of course I will give you some mustard seed! How much does the Blessed One need to work his miracle?"

"Just a little," Krisha Gautami said. Then, remembering suddenly: "But it must come from a house where no one has died."

Her neighbor turned back with a smile of pity. "Little Gautami, you know how many have died here. Just last month I lost my grandfather."

Krisha Gautami lowered her eyes, ashamed. "I'm sorry. I'll try next door."

But next door it was the same – and at the next house, and the next, and the house after that. Everyone wanted to help, but no one, even in the wealthiest homes, could meet that one simple condition. Death had come to all.

Finally Krisha Gautami understood. She took her child to the cremation ground and returned to the Compassionate Buddha.

"Sister," he greeted her, "did you bring me the mustard seed?"

"Blessed One," she said, falling at his feet, "I have had enough of this mustard seed. Just let me be your disciple!"

The Clay Lamp

One of the greatest admirers of the Buddha was King Bimbisara of Magadha. When he heard that the Buddha was approaching his capital, he hung the city with festive decorations and lined the main street with thousands of lamps in ornate holders, kept lit to honor the Buddha when he passed by.

In Bimbisara's capital lived an old woman who loved the Buddha deeply. She longed to take her own clay lamp and join the crowds that would line the road when he passed. The lamp was broken, but she was too poor to buy a finer one of brass. She made a wick from the edge of her sari, and the corner shopkeeper, knowing she had no money, poured a little oil into her lamp.

A stiff breeze had come up by the time she reached the street where the Buddha would pass, and the old woman knew there was not enough oil to last long. She did not light her lamp until the radiant figure of the Buddha came into view at the city gates.

The wind rose, and King Bimbisara must have watched in agony as a sudden gust extinguished all his lamps. When the Buddha passed, only one light remained burning: a broken clay lamp which an old woman guarded with both hands.

The Buddha stopped in front of her. As she knelt to receive his blessing, he turned to his disciples. "Take note of this woman! As long as spiritual disciplines are practiced with this kind of love and dedication, the light of the world will never go out."

The Last Entry into Nirvana

For over forty years the Buddha walked the length and breadth of north India, and throughout the rigors of a mendicant's life he was careful to keep his body fit. But in his eightieth year he fell so seriously ill that Ananda and some of the other brothers feared he might die.

Through the pain and fever, however, the Buddha's mind remained clear. He wrestled with death, and after a while the illness abated and strength returned.

"I wept," Ananda confessed, "for I was afraid you might leave us. But I remembered that you had left no instructions for us to follow if you were gone."

"If anyone believes that the Order would fail without his guidance," the Buddha replied drily, "that person surely should leave careful instructions. For my part, I know that the Order will not fail without my guidance. Why should I leave instructions? Be a refuge unto yourselves, Ananda. Be a lamp unto yourselves. Rely on yourselves and on nothing else. Hold fast to the dharma as your lamp, hold fast to the dharma as your refuge, and you shall surely reach nirvana, the highest good, the highest goal, if that is your deepest desire."

The next day the Buddha asked Ananda to summon all the monks in Vaishali. When all had gathered he spoke to them briefly, urging them to follow the path he had taught them with diligence and care, so that it might safely guide others for thousands of years. "Remember, brothers, all things that have come into being have to come to an end. Strive for the goal with all your heart. Within three months, he who has come this way to teach you will enter nirvana for the last time."

"For I will tell you," he confided later to Ananda, "that Mara has appeared to me again, as I have not seen him since the day I attained nirvana. 'You may rejoice now,' I told him, 'for this body will soon leave your kingdom.' Borne down under the weight of eighty years, Ananda, it creaks and groans like an ancient cart that has to have constant care to go on. Only in deep meditation am I at peace.

"But, Ananda, you must know that I will never leave you. How can I go anywhere? This body is not me. Unlimited by the body, unlimited by the mind, a Buddha is infinite and measureless, like the vast ocean or the canopy of sky. I live in the dharma I have given you, Ananda, which is closer to you than your own heart, and the dharma will never die."

On the following day the Buddha, looking back on the city of Vaishali for the last time, left with his disciples for Kusinara. But his health had not fully returned. On the way he rested in the mango grove of a lay follower named Chunda, who served the Buddha and his disciples with an elaborate meal. Again the Buddha's body was seized by pain. Again he subdued it, rousing the others to continue on their journey.

After some time he stopped along the road and asked Ananda to spread a robe beneath a tree for him to rest on. While he lay there, a man came to speak with him and left so impressed that he became a disciple. When he returned, he presented the Buddha with a new robe. Ananda, helping him to put it on, was struck by a change in his appearance. "How your face and skin shine, Blessed One! The gold of their radiance dulls even the saffron of this robe."

"There are two occasions when a Buddha's face and skin shine so," replied the Buddha gently: "when he first enters nirvana, and when he is about to enter nirvana for the last time."

Later that same day they arrived at Kusinara. There in a grove of sal trees the Buddha told Ananda to prepare him a bed, "for I am suffering, Ananda, and desire to lie down." He stretched himself out in what is called the lion posture, lying on his right side with one hand supporting his head, as we can still see him represented in the statues and carvings that depict his last hours.

He sent Ananda into the city of Kusinara to announce that he would shed his body during the third watch of the night, so that those who so desired could come and see him for the last time. They came with their whole households, in such great numbers that Ananda had to present them to the Buddha not individually but family by family.

When only the monks of the Order remained, the Buddha asked if anyone had a doubt or question about the Way. All were silent. The Buddha was satisfied. "Then I exhort you, brothers: remember, all things that come into being must pass away. Strive earnestly!"

They were his last words. Entering into deep meditation, he passed into nirvana for the last time.

THE STAGES OF ENLIGHTENMENT

Despite the Buddha's extraordinary capabilities, we must accept his own testimony that until the night of his enlightenment he saw life essentially the way the rest of us do. Yet after that experience he lived in a world where concepts like time and space, causality, personality, death, all mean something radically different. What happened to turn ordinary ways of seeing inside out?

In the Vinaya Pitaka (III.4) the Buddha left a concise map of his journey to nirvana – a description of the course of his meditation that night, couched in the kind of language a brilliant clinician might use in the lecture hall. In Buddhism the stages of this journey are called the "four *dhyanas*," from the Sanskrit word for meditation, which later passed into Japanese as *zen*. Scholars sometimes treat passage through the four dhyanas as a peculiarly Buddhist experience, but the Buddha's description tallies not only with Hindu authorities like Patanjali but also with Western mystics like John of the Cross, Teresa of Avila, Augustine, and Meister Eckhart. What the Buddha is giving us is something of universal application: a precise account of levels of awareness beneath the everyday waking state.

On that night, he tells us, he seated himself for meditation with the resolve not to get up again until he had attained his goal. Then, he continues,

I roused unflinching determination, focused my attention, made my body calm and motionless and my mind concentrated and one-pointed.

Standing apart from all selfish urges and all states of mind harmful to spiritual progress, I entered the first meditative state, where the mind, though not quite free from divided and diffuse thought, experiences lasting joy.

By putting an end to divided and diffuse thought, with my mind stilled in one-pointed absorption, I entered the second meditative state quite free from any wave of thought, and experienced the lasting joy of the unitive state.

As that joy became more intense and pure, I entered the third meditative state, becoming conscious in the very depths of the unconscious. Even my body was flooded with that joy of which the noble ones say, "They live in abiding joy who have stilled the mind and are fully awake."

Then, going beyond the duality of pleasure and pain and the whole field of memory-making forces in the mind, I dwelt at last in the fourth meditative state, utterly beyond the reach of thought, in that realm of complete purity which can be reached only through detachment and contemplation.

This was my first successful breaking forth, like a chick breaking out of its shell. . . .

This last quiet phrase is deadly. Our everyday life, the Buddha is suggesting, is lived within an eggshell. We have no more idea of what life is really like than a chicken has before it hatches. Excitement and depression, fortune and misfortune, pleasure and pain, are storms in a tiny, private, shell-bound realm which we take to be the whole of existence.

Yet we can break out of this shell and enter a new world. For a moment the Buddha draws aside the curtain of space and time and tells us what it is like to see into another dimension. When I read these words I remember listening to the far-off voice of Neil Armstrong that evening in 1969, telling us what it felt like to stand on the moon and look up at the earth floating in a sea of stars. The Buddha's voice reaches us from no distance at all, yet from a place much more remote. He is at the center of consciousness, beyond the thinking apparatus itself. As in some science fiction story, he has slipped through a kind of black hole into a parallel universe and returned to tell the rest of us what lies outside the boundaries of the mind.

To capture this vision will require many metaphors. Like snapshots of the same scene from different angles, they will sometimes appear inconsistent. This should present no problem to the modern mind. We are used to physicists presenting us with exotic and conflicting models – phenomena described as both particles and waves, parallel futures where something both takes place and does not, universes that are finite but unbounded. The mathematics behind these models is the best that imagination can do. And we laymen are satisfied: we cannot check the mathematics, but we are quite content to get an intuitive sense of what such radical ideas mean. Let us give the Buddha the same credence. Beneath the simple verses of the Dhammapada he will show us a universe every bit as fascinating as Bohr's or Einstein's.

The Buddha's dry description of the four dhyanas hides the fact that traversing them is a nearly impossible achievement. Even to enter the first dhyana requires years of dedicated, sustained, systematic effort, the kind of practice that turns an ordinary athlete into a champion.

This is an apt comparison, for the word the Buddha chose for "right effort" is one that is used for disciplined athletic training in general and gymnastics in particular. When the Buddha mentions with what determination he sat down for meditation that night, I remember the look I have seen on the face of championship athletes waiting to launch the performance that will win them an Olympic gold medal. They have trained their body for years, sharpened their concentration, unified their will, and that moment they have one thing on their mind and one thing only. Nothing less is required for meditation. Behind the Buddha's apparently effortless passage through deeper states of consciousness lie years of the most arduous training.

The First Dhyana

When a lover of music listens to a concert, she

is likely to close her eyes. If you call her name or touch her on the shoulder, she may not even notice. Attention has been withdrawn from her other senses and is concentrated in her hearing. The same thing happens as meditation deepens, except that attention is withdrawn from all the senses and turned inward. Western mystics call this "recollection," a literal translation of what the Buddha calls "right attention." No one has given a better comparison than St. Teresa: attention returns from the outside world, she says, like bees returning to the hive, and gathers inside in intense activity to make honey. Sound, touch, and so on are still perceived, but they make very little impression, almost as if the senses have been disconnected.

Gradually, as the quiet settles in, we realize we are in a new world. For a while we cannot see. Like moviegoers entering a dark theater for a matinée, our eyes are still dazzled by the glare from outside. To learn to move about in this world takes time. A blind man has hearing and touch to help direct him from place to place, but in the unconscious, with the senses closed down, there are no landmarks that one can recognize.

At this level we begin to see how the mind works. Cut off from its accustomed sensory input, it runs around looking for something to stimulate it. The Buddha specifies two aspects of this: "divided thought," the ordinary two-track mind, trying to keep attention on two things at once, and "diffuse thought," the mind's tendency to wander. The natural direction of this movement is outward, toward the sensations of experience. To turn inward, this movement has to be reversed. Throughout the first dhyana the centrifugal force of the thinking process is gradually absorbed as attention is recalled.

Ordinarily, thought follows a course of stimulus and response. Some event, whether in the world or in the mind, sets off a chain of associations, and attention follows. To descend through the personal unconscious, we need concentration that cannot be broken by any sensory attraction or emotional response – in a word, mastery over our senses and our likes and dislikes. Most people work through the first dhyana by developing this kind of self-control during the day. The Buddha, however, has covered this ground already. His passions are mastered and his mind one-pointed. When he sits down to meditate, he crosses this region of the mind without distraction.

This is only the first leg of a very long journey, but even in itself it is a rare achievement. The concentration it requires will bring success in any field, along with a deep sense of well-being, security, and a quiet joy in living. No great flashes of insight come at this level, but you do begin to see connections between personal problems and their deeper causes, and with this comes the will to make changes in your life.

The Second Dhyana

To talk about regions of the mind like this, I confess, is a little misleading. Between the first and second dhyanas there is no demarcation line. Both are areas of what might be called the personal unconscious, that sector of the mind in which lie the thoughts, feelings, habits, and experiences peculiar to oneself as an individual. In the second dhyana, however, concentration is much deeper, and the demands of the senses – to taste, hear, touch, smell, or see, to experience some sensation or other – have become much less shrill. The quiet of meditation is unassailed by the outside world. Distractions can still break the thread of concentration, but much less easily; gradually they seem more and more distant.

Here the struggle for self-mastery moves to a significantly deeper level. Associations, desires, and thoughts generated by the preoccupations of the day leave behind their disguises of rational, unselfish behavior and appear for what they are. The ego has retreated to more basic demands: the claims of "I" and "mine." Here, to make progress, we become eager for opportunities to go against self-will, especially in personal relationships. There is no other way to gain detachment from the self-centered conditioning that burdens every human being. The Buddha calls this "swimming against the current": the concerted, deliberate effort to dissolve self-interest in the desire to serve a larger whole, when eons of conditioning have programmed us to serve ourselves first.

This is painful, but with the pain comes satisfaction in mastering some of the strongest urges in the human personality. When you sit for meditation you descend steadily, step by step, into the depths of the unconscious. The experience is very much like what deep-sea divers describe when they lower themselves into the black waters hundreds of feet down. The world of everyday experience seems as remote as the ocean's surface, and you feel immense pressure in your head, as if you were immersed under the weight of a sea of consciousness. The thread of concentration is your lifeline then. If it breaks, you can lose your way in these dark depths.

Here all the mind's attention – even what ordinarily goes to subconscious urges and preoccupations – is being absorbed in a single focus. This seemingly simple state comes spontaneously only to men and women of great genius, and it contains immense power. The rush of the thinking process has been slowed to a crawl, each moment of thought under control. The momentum of the mind has been gathered into great reserves of potential energy, as an object gathers when lifted against the pull of gravity.

In these depths comes a revolutionary realization: thought is not continuous. Instead of being a smooth, unbroken stream, the thinking process is more like the flow of action in a movie: only a series of stills, passing our eyes faster than we can perceive.

This idea is one of the most abstract in Buddhism, and

movies make such a concrete illustration that I feel sure the Buddha would have appreciated having a reel of film around to show intellectuals like Malunkyaputra. "You wouldn't say a movie is unreal, would you?" he might ask. "But the appearance of continuity is unreal, and confusing a movie with reality is not right understanding."

Most of us find it easy to get involved in certain kinds of movies. We get caught up in the action and forget ourselves, and our body and mind respond as if we were there on the screen. The heart races, blood pressure goes up, fists clench, and the mind gets excited and jumps to conclusions, just as if we were actually experiencing what is happening to the hero or heroine. The Buddha would say, "You *are* experiencing it: and that is the way you experience life, too."

This may sound heartless, as if he is saying that excitement and tragedy are no more than a celluloid illusion. Not at all. What he means is that as human beings, our responses should not be automatic; we should be able to choose. When the mind is excited, we jump into a situation and do whatever comes automatically, which often only makes things worse. If the mind is calm, we see clearly and don't get emotionally entangled in events around us, leaving us free to respond with compassion.

Most of us have never thought much about the mechanics of film projection, so we are surprised to learn that every moment of image on the screen is followed by a moment of no-image when the screen is dark. We do not perceive these moments of emptiness. Action stimulates the mind; no-action bores it. Attention follows the desire to be stimulated and skips over what the mind finds meaningless. The power of imagination jumps the gaps between images, holding them together in our mind. Only when the projector is slowed down do we begin to see the flicker of the screen.

When this happens in a movie, our interest wanes. Our attention is not powerful enough to hold together in a continuous flow images that are broken by more than a fraction of a second. Such a feat requires the concentration of genius. I think it was Keynes who said that Newton had the capacity to hold a single problem in the focus of his mind for days, weeks, even years, until it was solved. That is just what is required at this depth in meditation. The thinking process is slowed until you can almost see each thought pass by, yet instead of one thought following another without rhyme or reason, the mind has such power that the focus of concentration is not disturbed.

At this depth in consciousness, the sense world and even the notion of personal identity is very far away. Asleep to one's body, asleep even to the thoughts, feelings, and desires that we think of as ourselves, we are nevertheless intensely awake in an inner world – deep in the unconscious, near the very threshold of personality.

The Third Dhyana

If thought is discontinuous, we want to ask, what is between two thoughts? The answer is, nothing. A thought is like a wave in consciousness; between two thoughts there is no movement in the mind at all. Consciousness itself is like a still lake, clear, calm, and full of joy.

When the thought-process has been slowed to a crawl in meditation, there comes a time when – without warning – the movie of the mind stops and you get a glimpse right through the mind into deeper consciousness. This is called *bodhi*, and it comes like a blinding glimpse of pure light accompanied by a flood of joy.

This experience is not what Zen Buddhists call "no-mind." It is only, if I may coin a term, "no-thought." The thinking process has such immense momentum that even at this depth, concentration has power enough to stop it only for an instant before it starts up again. But the joy of this experience is so intense that all your desires for life's lesser satisfactions merge in the deep, driving desire to do everything possible to stop the mind again.

This point marks the threshold between the second and third dhyanas. Crossing this threshold is one of the most difficult challenges in the spiritual journey. You feel blocked by an impenetrable wall. Bodhi is a glimpse of the other side, as you get when you drop a quarter into the telescope near the Golden Gate Bridge and the shutter snaps open for a two-minute look at sea lions frolicking on the rocks. But these first experiences of bodhi are over in an instant, leaving you so eagerly frustrated that you are willing to do anything to get through. You feel your way along that wall from one end to the other looking for a break, and finally you realize that there isn't any. And you just start chipping away. It requires the patience of someone trying to wear down the Himalayas with a piece of silk – and you feel you are making about as much progress.

This is a rarefied world. Like the outside world, personal identity is far away. You feel as if the wall between yourself and the rest of creation were paper-thin. If you are to go further, this wall has to fall. For on the opposite side lies the collective unconscious: not necessarily what Jung meant when he coined the term, but what the Buddha calls "storehouse consciousness," the strata of the mind shared by every individual creature. Here are stored the seeds of our evolutionary heritage, the race-old instincts, drives, urges, and experiences of a primordial past. To dive into these dark waters and stay conscious, you have to take off your individual personality and leave it on the shore.

Paradoxically, this cannot be accomplished by any amount of will and drive associated with the individual self. It is not done just in meditation but during the day. Doing "good works" is not enough; the mental state is crucial. There must be no taint of "I" or "mine" in what you do, no self-interest, only your best effort to see yourself in all.

One way to explain this is that karma has to be cleared before you can cross the wall. All the momentum of the thinking process comes from the residue of karma. To clear our accounts, we have to absorb whatever comes to us with kindness, calmness, courage, and compassion. Karma is not really erased; its negative entries are balanced with positive ones in a flood of selfless service.

When the books of karma are almost closed, the Buddha says, you "come to that place where one grieves no more." Then you see that the mistakes of your past and their karmic payback were part of a pattern of spiritual growth stretching over many lives. Once paid for, those mistakes are no longer yours. They are the life history of a person made up of thoughts, desires, and motives that are gone. The karma of those thoughts applied to the old person; it cannot stick to the new. Then the past carries no guilt and no regrets. You have learned what was to be learned. Recollecting past errors is like picking up a book about someone else, reading a page or two, and then putting it back on the shelf.

You may wait and wait at this threshold, consumed in a patient impatience, doing everything possible during the day to allow you to break through in your next meditation. This can go on for days, months, even years; it is not really in your hands. But then, suddenly, the mind-process stops and stays stopped. You slip through, and the waters of the collective unconscious close over your head.

Beyond this, words are useless. Time stops with the mind, and many physiological processes are almost suspended. But there is an intense, unbroken flood of joy to which even the body and nervous system respond.

This experience cannot last. Like a diver, you have to come up for air. But unity has left an indelible imprint. Never again will you believe yourself a separate creature, a finite physical entity that was born to die. You know firsthand that you are inseparable from the whole of creation, and you are charged by the power of this experience to serve all life.

The Fourth Dhyana

Even this is not journey's end. Like a traveler returning from another country, you remember clearly what you have seen in bodhi; yet during the day, the everyday world closes in around you again. Such is the power of the mind that the mundane soon seems real, and unity something far away. In the third dhyana the conditioned instincts of the mind are stilled but not destroyed. They remain like seeds, ready to sprout when you return to surface awareness. The experience of unity has to be repeated over and over until those seeds are burned out, so that they can never sprout again.

We know what power a compulsive desire can have at the

surface of the mind. In these depths, that power is magnified a thousand times. You feel as if you are standing on the floor of an ocean where no light has ever reached, buffeted by currents you cannot understand. Then you *know* that the mind is a field of forces.

But that does not tell you how to deal with these forces. In the unconscious, the will does not operate. Yet to make progress you have to learn to make it operate, so that you can harness the power of the unconscious in everyday life. That is the challenge of crossing the third dhyana, compared with which skydiving and whitewater racing are armchair exploits.

Your goal is to reach such a depth that even in dreams the awareness of unity remains unbroken. Then every corner of the mind is flooded with light. The partitions fall; consciousness is unified from surface to seabed. You are awake on the very floor of the unconscious, and life is a seamless whole.

This is nirvana. The seeds of a separate personality have been burned out; they will not germinate again. When you return to the surface of consciousness, you pick up the appearance of personality and slip it on again. But it is the personality of a new man, a new woman, purified of separateness and reborn in the love of all life.

Those who achieve this exalted state, the Buddha says simply, have done what has to be done. They have fulfilled the purpose of life. They may be born again, if they choose, in order to help others to attain the goal. But this is their choice, not a matter of compulsion. Therefore, the Buddha says, this body is their last. *Samsara*, the ceaseless round of birth and death, has no beginning, but it has an end: nirvana. Nirvana has a beginning, but once attained it has no end.

As a word, *nirvana* is negative. It means "to blow out," as one would extinguish a fire, and the Buddha often describes it as putting out, cooling, or quenching the fires of self-will and selfish passion. But the force of the word is entirely positive. Like the English word *flawless*, it expresses perfection as the absence of any fault. Perfection, the Buddha implies, is our real nature. All we have to do is remove the self-centeredness that covers it.

Someone once asked the Buddha skeptically, "What have you gained through meditation?"

The Buddha replied, "Nothing at all."

"Then, Blessed One, what good is it?"

"Let me tell you what I *lost* through meditation: sickness, anger, depression, insecurity, the burden of old age, the fear of death. That is the good of meditation, which leads to nirvana."

What draws one back from this sublime state? The separate personality is lost, yet we cannot say nothing remains. There is a kind of shadow which the Buddha wears, clothing him in humanity, yet it is so thin that the radiance of infinity transfigures him. Siddhartha dissolved in the fourth dhyana, and one called the Buddha returned from it; that is all we can say.

There have been mystics East and West who did not care to

return, who let their bodies go rather than leave this blissful state. But the Buddha was not of this kind. He had been born for a purpose – not just to attain nirvana for himself, but to bring it to all – and he was not willing to leave until that purpose was fulfilled. Even at these depths, where personality is gone, a will remains that is unbreakable.

THE BUDDHA'S UNIVERSE

The story of the Buddha captures the heart of this luminous teacher who, in his own words, loved the world as a mother loves her only child. But there is more to the Buddha than his heart. As with a good physician, behind that immense compassion is the penetrating vision of a scientific mind.

It is this scientific outlook that I now want to touch on, for it produced a worldview of very contemporary appeal. Some years ago the BBC produced a brilliant television series called *Einstein's Universe*, showing how the world would look if we could see the effects of relativity. It is a fascinating realm, full of bent rays of light, warps in time, and black holes in the fabric of space itself. Just as fascinating is the Buddha's universe: his view of life after attaining nirvana.

Relativity and quantum theory, in fact, provide excellent illustrations of this strange world, so contrary to common sense. In the Buddha's universe a personal, separate self is an illusion, just as substance is an illusion to the atomic physicist. Distinctions between an "outside world" and an "inner realm" of the mind are arbitrary. Everything in human experience takes place in one field of forces, which comprises both matter and mind. Thought and physical events act and react upon each other as naturally and inescapably as do matter and energy. But the basis of the natural world is not physical. As Einstein described matter and energy solely in terms of the geometry of space-time, the Buddha describes matter, energy, and mental events as the structure of a fabric we can call consciousness. His universe is a process in continuous change – a seething sea of primordial energy, of which the mind and the physical world are only different aspects.

Personality

Set the Buddha down on another world, like Armstrong and Aldrin on the moon, and he doesn't stand around marveling; he immediately starts ferreting out secrets. Instead of basking in bliss on the night of his enlightenment, he looks around on the seabed of the unconscious and begins tracing connections.

In physics, the realization that light is not continuous led to a new view of the world. Much in the Buddha's worldview stems from a similar discovery about thought. Like light, we can say, thought consists of quanta, discrete bursts of energy. The Buddha referred to these thought-quanta as *dharmas* – not *dharma* in the sense of the underlying law of life, but

in another sense meaning something like "a state of being."
When the thinking process slows considerably, it is seen to
be a series of such dharmas, each unconnected with those
before or after. One dharma arises and subsides in a moment;
then another arises to replace it, and it too dies away. Each
moment is *now,* and it is the succession of such moments that
creates the sense of time.

The Buddha would say these dharmas come from nowhere
and they return to nowhere. Mind is a series of thought-
moments as unconnected as the successive images of a movie.
A movie screen does not really connect one moment's image
to the next, and similarly there is no substrate beneath the
mind to connect thoughts. The mind *is* the thoughts, and only
the speed of thinking creates the illusion that there is something continuous and substantial.

For the personal ego, which seems so real and consid-
ers its satisfactions so all-important, this does not add up to
an attractive self-image. The bundle of thoughts, memories,
desires, fears, urges, anxieties, and aspirations that we think
of as ourselves is largely an illusion: a lot of separate mental
events temporarily associated with a physical body, but nothing that anyone could call a whole.

Even in such abstract thinking, the Buddha remains in
touch with his audience. Everyone would have been familiar with the village marketplace, where vendors spread their
wares on mats for passersby to see. When someone wants

spices for that night's dinner, the spice-seller takes a banana leaf, doles out little heaps of coriander, ginger, and the like, wraps them up in the leaf, and ties the bundle with a banana string. That is how the Buddha describes personality: a blend of five *skandhas* or "heaps" of ingredients like these piles of spices in their banana-leaf wrapper. These ingredients are *rupa*, form, *vedana*, sensation or feeling, *samjna*, perception, *samskara*, the forces or impulses of the mind, and *vijnana*, consciousness. Without reference to an individual self or soul, the Buddha says that birth is the coming together of these aggregates; death is their breaking apart.

"Form" is the body, with which most of us identify ourselves and others. It is the sameness of body from day to day that provides the continuity of who we are. When the body dies, what is left? Even in an afterlife, we can't really imagine ourselves without form.

For the Buddha, however, this physical identification is as ridiculous as mistaking the dinner spices for the leaf in which they are wrapped. The body is only a wrapper. Most of a person is mind, which is a blend every bit as particular as a physical body is. We identify a person by referring to his big hands, his dimple, her fingerprints, the mole on his left cheek. The Buddha would refer to a person's mindprint: his big ego, her tender heart, her fondness for chocolate, his fear of being wrong. But these characteristics are not fixed. The blend is subtly but constantly changing in response to what we think and experience, just as biologists say the physical body itself is constantly changing at the chemical level. The skandhas are not substances but processes, and the mind, in Buddhist terms, is a field of forces.

The second skandha is sensation or feeling. When we identify with the body, it is only natural that we identify also with the sensations it experiences, whether pleasant, painful, or neutral.

Many people, for example, register a pleasant sensation when they smell fresh coffee brewing. They will tell you that coffee has a pleasant smell, as if this were as factual as saying it has a brown color. But these attributions are personal, conditioned by past experience and association. In my native state of Kerala, South India, if people see you drinking coffee they are likely to ask, "Aren't you feeling well?" Kerala is tea country; coffee is something you would drink only if you were sick. In reality, the smell of brewing coffee is neither pleasant nor unpleasant; it is just a smell. But when we identify ourselves with the skandhas, we cannot usually see this; we identify with our response.

The third skandha is usually called perception, but more accurately it is the act of naming the sensation experience. If the nose reports a deep, strong aroma of roasted beans, the next thing the mind does is label it: "Coffee!" That name carries all the associations our conditioning to coffee has built up for us, depending on our culture and context.

The fourth skandha is the strong, instinctive, gut-level reactions triggered by this naming. In the case of coffee, the Buddha would say, we react not so much to the coffee itself as to our perception or label of it: the conditioned habit of liking or disliking. The Sanskrit name for this is *samskara*, which means literally "that which is intensely done." Samskaras are thought, speech, or behavior motivated by the desire to get some experience for oneself. We can think of samskaras as grooves of conditioning, compulsive desires. It is this skandha which prompts action – or, more accurately, which prompts karma, for "action" here includes thought.

A person with a strong coffee samskara will smell it brewing and think, "I want some!" Someone from Kerala might say, "How unappealing!" Whatever the label, if we act on a samskara it becomes stronger. The conditioning is reinforced, making it more likely that we will act on that samskara the next time. Samskaras are the key to character, but their root is deep below the level of conscious awareness. We see what they do, but we have very little control over the forces themselves.

The last skandha is *vijnana*, "consciousness": the appropriation of each unit of experience to the mass of conditioning formed by the experiences of the past. Vijnana is like a river, carrying the accumulated karma of all previous thought and action. When I smell coffee, the sensation may awaken a coffee samskara. If it does, my response to that samskara becomes one more piece of flotsam in the stream of consciousness, joining the experiences which represent the whole history of my contact with coffee, beginning with the first time I smelled it brewing.

It is this stream of consciousness that we identify with a self, because its experiences seem to have happened to a particular individual. But according to the Buddha, this self is only imagined, superimposed on momentary, unconnected mental events. If the mind is compared to a movie, vijnana is like the series of clicks of the camera shutter: "This frame (and nothing outside it) is I, this is I, this is I." The Buddha would ask, "*What* is I?" What we see is simply not there. We see the images flash by and think we are watching Clark Gable; but in reality, of course, we are watching no one, only a series of stills.

The World

This is unsettling enough, but it is only the beginning. The opening verse of the Dhammapada takes us the next step: "Our life is shaped by our mind, for we become what we think."

These simple lines are both the subtlest and the most practical in the Dhammapada. The words are too rich for any translation to convey their full meaning. Literally they say, "Mind is the forerunner of all dharmas. All follow the mind; all are made out of mind."

Dharmas has a double edge here: it means, at the same

time, both "things" and "thoughts." To the Buddha, everything is a dharma, a mental event. We don't really experience
the world, he observes; we experience constructs in the mind
made up of information from the senses. This information is
already a kind of code. We don't actually see things, for example; we interpret as separate objects a mass of electrochemical
impulses received by the brain. And of course this information covers only a narrow range of sensibility, limited to what
the senses can register. But from this scanty data the mind
makes a whole world.

We have grown used to the idea that there is much more
"out there" than we can be aware of. But this is not what the
Buddha is saying. He drops the convention of "out there"
altogether. Everything in experience is mind. What we call
"things" are objects in consciousness: not that they are imagi-
nary, but their characteristics are mental constructions. Like
the other skandhas, form is a category of mind.

As I was driving to the beach for a walk, it struck me that
from far off, the sand appears solid. Only when we stand on
it and touch it can we see it is really billions of particles. The
same is true even with things that are "really" solid, such as a
boulder at the water's edge. Physicists resolve even subatomic
particles into energy, making "substance" a tool for everyday communication rather than a description of reality. Similarly, the Buddha reduces all experience – of things and of
ourselves – to dharmas. Deep in consciousness, a common-

sense experience like a beautiful sunset resolves into skandha-events like "sight-contact of color patterns accompanied by pleasurable sensation." There is no self in such events, and no real distinction between observer and observed.

The Buddha, I think, would not have been surprised by the discoveries of this century which turned classical physics upside down. The essential discontinuity in nature observed by quantum physicists follows naturally from the Buddha's experience of the discontinuity of thought. So does the idea that time is discontinuous, which may find a place in physics also.

We have to be very careful of misunderstanding here, for the Buddha is not saying that the physical world is a figment of imagination. That would imply a "real" world to compare with, and this *is* the real world. We are not "making it up," but neither are we misperceiving a reality "out there" where things *are* solid and individuals are separate. What the Buddha is telling us is precisely parallel to what the quantum physicists say: when we examine the universe closely, it dissolves into discontinuity and a flux of fields of energy. But in the Buddha's universe the mind-matter duality is gone; these are fields in consciousness.

When Einstein talked about clocks slowing down in a powerful gravitational field, or when Heisenberg said we can determine either the momentum or the position of an electron but not both, most physicists felt a natural tendency to treat these as apparent aberrations, like the illusion that a stick bends when placed in a glass of water. It took decades for physicists to accept that there is no "real" universe, like the real stick, to refer to without an observer. Clocks really do slow down and electrons really are indeterminable; that is the way the universe actually is. Similarly, the Buddha would say, this universe we talk of *is* made of mind. There is no "real" world-in-itself apart from our perceiving it. This doesn't make physical reality any less physical; it only reminds us that what we see in the world is shaped by the structure of consciousness.

This has radical implications, one of which is that "mind" and "matter" are different ways of looking at the same thing. Today we are used to thinking of matter as "frozen energy." Mind too can be considered energy in a different form. You may remember Bohr's principle of complementarity: to get a whole picture of light, we have to describe it as waves and as particles at the same time. Similarly, the Buddha would say, if we look at experience one way – in the ordinary waking state – we see physical reality; if we look at it another way, we see mind. In profound meditation, one goes beyond sensory appearance and eventually beyond the very structure of the phenomenal world: time, space, causality. Time stops; there is only the present moment. Then everything is pure energy, a sea of light.

We want to ask, "Matter and mind are different aspects of

what 'same thing'? It's all very well to say 'consciousness,' but what does that mean?" Like most quantum physicists, however, the Buddha doesn't try to explain further. The question doesn't make sense. It can't be answered without creating confusion and contradiction, and anyway it is unnecessary. When you ask a physicist what "ultimate reality" is like, he or she is likely to reply, "We can describe accurately, and that's enough. The laws *are* the reality." The Buddha does the same. He says, "This is the way the universe is. If you want to know more, go see for yourself."

This is not heady philosophy; it has some surprisingly practical implications. One is that we see life as we are. The world of our experience is partly of our own making, colored and distorted by the past experiences that each person identifies with a personal ego. My relationship with you is not with you as you see yourself, but with you as I see you: a waxworks creation in my mind. As a result, two people can share the same house and literally live in different worlds.

If these ideas were better understood, they could make our planet a very different place. We have a story in India about two men, one high-minded and generous, the other very selfish, who were sent to foreign lands and asked to tell what kind of people they found there. The first reported that he found people basically good at heart, not very different from those at home. The second man felt envious hearing this, for in the place he visited everyone was selfish, scheming, and cruel.

Both, of course, were describing the same land. "We see as we are," and our foreign policy follows what we see. Those who see themselves surrounded by a hostile world preparing for war tend to make that vision a reality.

It follows that when we change ourselves, we have already begun to change the world. Heisenberg taught physicists that in subatomic realms, the observer affects the observation. The way we ask an experimental question determines the kind of answer we will get. In the Buddha's universe this is true for all experience. If a hostile person learns to slow down his thinking enough to see how much of what provokes him is projected by his own mind, his world changes, and so does his behavior – which, in turn, changes the world for those around him. "Little by little," the Buddha says, "we make ourselves good, as a bucket fills with water drop by drop." Little by little, too, we change the world we live in. Even the grand earthshaking events of history have their origins in individual thought.

Karma, Death, and Birth

Placing physical phenomena and mind in the same field may seem confusing at first, but like Einstein's marriage of matter and energy, it leads to a view of the world that is elegant in its simplicity. Much in the Buddha's universe, in fact, can be understood as a generalization of physical laws to a larger sphere.

The law of karma, for example, which seems so exotic when mind and matter are relegated to different worlds, simply states that cause and effect apply universally and that the effect is of the nature of the cause. Every event, mental or physical, has to have effects, whether in the mind, in action, or in both – and each such effect becomes a cause itself.

To the Buddha, the universe is a vast sea where any stone thrown raises ripples among billions of other ripples. Karma raises ripple-effects within personality and without, for both are in the same field of forces. When we pursue our own self-interest, we are adding to a sea of selfish behavior in which we too live. Sooner or later, the consequences cannot help but come back to us.

Karma is stored in the mind. What we call personality is made up of karma, for it is the accumulation of everything we have done and said and thought. So karma follows wherever we go. "Fly in the sky, burrow in the ground," says the Buddha, "you cannot escape the consequences of your actions." You can run, but you cannot hide. All of us have karmic scores to settle, a book of debits and credits that is constantly growing.

The end of the body cannot clear these accounts, for although the skandhas of personality come apart, I-consciousness is not destroyed. Thus we come logically to the last theme of the Buddha's universe: the cycle of death and rebirth.

Here again let me illustrate from Einstein, who proposed

that instead of talking only about particles, we talk also about fields. At very small distances, the field we call an electron is so intense that it behaves like a particle. At a greater distance the strength of the field drops off rapidly, but strictly speaking it never vanishes. For practical purposes, it has local definition. But a universe of such fields is a whole, not a collection of parts, and to speak of particular fields as separate is like isolating currents and whirlpools in the ocean: sometimes practical, but superficial.

To the Buddha, the field of forces we think of as personality is similar; it can be talked about meaningfully, yet it is not separate from the rest of life. As a subatomic particle seems to form out of states of energy and then dissolves into energy again; individual creatures come into physical existence and pass from it again and again in the ceaseless process called *samsara*, the flux of life. However, while the creation or destruction of an electron may be a matter of chance, I-consciousness reenters physical existence according to the karma that remains to be worked out. We choose the context in which we are born – not consciously, of course, but by the sum of our previous actions and desires.

Think of the way an oak tree propagates itself. An acorn ripens and falls, germinates when physical conditions are right, and grows into another oak. We see two separate oaks, but on the atomic level a biologist can trace a continuous flow of energy from tree to acorn to tree. In a similar way, the

Buddha would trace the individual packet of forces we call personality. When these forces are expressed physically, that is the interval between birth and death. But after death, just as the basic characteristics of the oak tree lie dormant in the acorn's genetic code, the forces of an individual personality still cohere, waiting to burst into life again when the proper conditions are present.

Personally, I find this no more miraculous than what the acorn does. A seed does not contribute much materially to the plant it grows into; the material comes from the soil, sunlight, water, and air. What the seed contributes is information. It has the same DNA as every other living entity, but when its genes begin to be expressed, it pulls from the environment what is needed to make a plant of just a particular kind. We wonder at this, but we accept it because it is physical. The Buddha finds personality processes just as real.

Those who question him on this level of observation play a dangerous game, for no one is more relentlessly logical. If we object that what he calls a "person" is not the same from one life to the next, he will ask, "Are *you* the same from one day to the next?" We think of ourselves as the same individual who went to school in Des Moines many years ago, but what is the basis for such a claim? Our desires, aspirations, and opinions may all have changed; even our bones are not the same.

Yet, somehow, there is continuity. "I wasn't the same then," we object, "but that wasn't a different person either." The

Buddha replies, "That is the relationship between you in this life and 'you' in a past life: you are not the same, but neither are you different. Death is only the temporary end of a temporary phenomenon." To those who grasp this, death loses its fear. It is not the end, only a door into another room.

Nirvana

During the first watch of the night of his enlightenment, the Buddha tells us, he traced the personality known as Siddhartha Gautama back over many lives. In the second watch, he saw the world "as if in a spotless mirror" – the countless deaths and rebirths of other creatures, their context in life determined by the karma of past action. "And compassion welled up within him," for he saw only blind paths of stimulus and response: no understanding of the laws that govern what we call "fate," no awareness that we can take our lives into our own hands.

In the last hours before dawn, he focused his attention on how to break this chain of suffering once and for all.

The first link, he saw, is ignorance. Instead of seeing life as a flux, we insist on seeing what we want it to be, a collection of things and experiences with the power to satisfy. Instead of seeing our personality as it is – an impermanent process – we cling to what we want it to be, something real and separate and permanent. From this root ignorance arises *trishna*, the insistent craving for personal satisfaction. From trishna comes duhkha, the frustration and suffering that are the human condition.

With our glimpse into the Buddha's universe, it is clear why human grasping seemed to him so ignorant and blind. We are trying to get from life something that is not there – trying to find a real Clark Gable in a movie, trying to find some experience that will last. And what we are trying to hold on with isn't there either. We want to gratify a process with a process. The ego *cannot* be satisfied, and the more we try, the more we suffer.

But the frustration of this grasping, because it derives from ignorance, is not real. It is a shadow which can be dispelled by seeing life as it really is. The Buddha says succinctly, "This arising, that arises": whenever there is ignorance of life's nature, suffering has to follow. "This subsiding, that subsides": as self-will dies, we awaken to our real nature. Then personal sorrow comes to an end.

What is this real nature? Here the Buddha remains silent. He comes to us to point the way, to show a path, but he steadfastly refuses to limit with words what we will find.

Yet he does tell us that there is more to life than flux and process and the mechanical working out of karma. "There is something unborn, unbecome, not made and not compounded. If there were not, there would be no means of escape from what is born, become, made, and compounded." In the limitless sea of samsara, in the midst of change, there is an island, a farther shore, a realm of being that is utterly beyond the transient world in which we live: nirvana.

When the mind is stilled, the appearance of change and separateness vanishes and nirvana remains. It is *shunyata*, emptiness, only in that there is literally nothing there: "no-thing." But emptiness of process means fullness of being. Nirvana is *aroga*, freedom from all illness; *shiva*, happiness; *kshema*, security; *abhaya*, the absence of fear; *shanta*, peace of mind; *anashrava*, freedom from compulsions; *ajara*, untouched by age; *amata*, unaffected by death. It is, in sum, *parama sukha*, the highest joy.

Those who attain the island of nirvana can live thereafter in the sea of change without being swept away. They know what life is and know that there is something more. Lacking nothing, craving nothing, they stay in the world solely to help and serve. We cannot say they live without grief; it is their sensitiveness to the suffering of others that motivates their lives. But personal sorrow is gone. They live to give, and their capacity to go on giving is a source of joy so great that it cannot be measured against any sensation the world offers.

Without understanding this dimension, the Buddha's universe is an intellectually heady affair that offers little satisfaction to the heart. When we hear that our personality is no more real than a movie, we may feel dejected, abandoned in an alien universe. The Buddha replies gently, "You don't understand." If life were not a process, if thought were continuous, we would have no freedom of choice, no alternative to the human condition. It is because each thought is a moment of its own that we can change.

"Our life is shaped by our mind, for we become what we think." That is the essence of the Buddha's universe and the whole theme of the Dhammapada. If we can get hold of the thinking process, we can actually redo our personality, remake ourselves. Destructive ways of thinking can be rechanneled, constructive channels can be deepened, all through right effort and meditation. "As irrigators lead water to their fields, as archers make their arrows straight, as carpenters carve wood, the wise shape their lives."

"The universe is hostile," Wernher von Braun once said, "only when you do not know its laws. To those who know and obey, the universe is friendly." When understood, the Buddha's universe too is anything but alien and inhibiting. It is a world full of hope, where everything we need to do can be done and everything that matters is within human reach. It is a world where kindness, unselfishness, nonviolence, and compassion for all creatures achieve what self-interest and arrogance cannot. It is, simply, a world where any human being can be happy in goodness and the fullness of giving.

. We have the path to this world in the Dhammapada.

▯▮

THE DHAMMAPADA

▮▯

Translated by Eknath Easwaran

Chapter Introductions by Stephen Ruppenthal

A NOTE ON THE TEXT

Buddhist scriptures are divided into three pitakas or "baskets." By far the largest and most important of these is the Sutra Pitaka (in Pali, Sutta Pittaka) or "basket of discourses," which consists mostly of talks by the Buddha or one of his direct disciples. The Dhammapada, though not considered a sutra, is included in this collection. The other two collections are the Vinaya Pitaka or "basket of discipline," containing the rules of the monastic order, and the Abhidharma Pitaka or "basket of metaphysics," containing works analyzing the philosophy behind the Buddha's teachings.

The oldest version of this canon to have survived is in Pali, a vernacular descendant of Sanskrit. The Dhammapada is best known in its Pali form, and that is the version translated here. Buddhist terms, however, appear here in Sanskrit, because it is in Sanskrit rather than Pali – nirvana rather than nibbana, dharma rather than dhamma, karma rather than kamma, and so on – that these words have become familiar in the West, largely due to the influence of Mahayana Buddhism and particularly of Zen. For consistency, we have also kept the Sanskrit version of proper names, though Buddhist tradition often preserves the Pali as the more familiar form.

□: *Twin Verses & Vigilance*

THE SUTRAS OR discourses of the Buddha preserved in the Buddhist Pali canon were largely aimed at the monks and nuns of the Buddhist order. But the Dhammapada was meant for everyone. Its 423 verses are much more than wise aphorisms to be read and reflected over. They contain that part of the Buddha's teaching which can be grasped and put into practice by the greatest number of people, by following the disciplines of the Eightfold Path. Every reader knows that one book which becomes part of one's life means more than a thousand others. The Dhammapada was meant as such a book, and its method for transforming our lives is given right in the first chapter.

The title "Twin Verses" gives the cue: chapter 1 presents pairs of possibilities for human conduct, each leading to a different kind of destiny. There are ten verse pairs, and usually it is the negative possibility, the kind of conduct catering to conditioned human wants, that is presented first. Then comes the positive one, which runs contrary to human nature. The first alternative usually is easily accomplished and temporarily satisfying. The second, however, goes against the conditioning of the pleasure principle, and to implement it requires hard effort on the Eightfold Path. But in the long run, the sweet and easy way leads to more suffering; the hard way, to nirvana. The Buddha can only point the way (276); the hard choice we must make ourselves, again and again, until it becomes part of our personality.

The Buddha says later (290), "If one who enjoys a lesser happiness beholds a greater one, let him leave aside the lesser to gain the greater." This is the "greater happiness" – the second, more difficult path – which will come to any human being who recognizes the choice there is in every action, even in every thought, and has the will and discrimination to choose wisely. Robert Frost's famous lines from "The Road Not Taken" provide a model for the crossroads at which every human being stands:

> Two roads diverged in a wood, and I –
> I took the one less traveled by,
> And that has made all the difference.

Why can't a person just pass by the easy road and take "the one less traveled by" if it leads to permanent happiness? The obstacle is the mind. It is one's mental state that determines which of these possibilities a person will act on. The mind can be said to be a product of the human being's evolutionary drive to look out for oneself first. Its natural response to any situation is to take the easiest, least unpleasant course to personal fulfillment. The Buddha calls this swimming with the current, taking the easy path traveled by the many. To find happiness, one has to go *against* the current, against every selfish impulse.

Here one can see the dilemma the Buddha faced as a teacher: how will anyone believe that the hard way really leads to the happiness that all seek? In his experience of enlightenment, he had seen for himself that eternal principles operate in human affairs; hatred, for example, cannot put an end to hatred no matter what the circumstances or pretext (5). But how could he motivate others to act on these principles unless they experienced the truth for themselves? Like Jesus, the Buddha had to find ways to make things and events that everyone was familiar with reverberate with the power of what he had understood in the depths of meditation.

Nowhere is this clearer than in the Dhammapada, where deep, subtle truths take on the garb of common village scenes familiar to the audiences the Buddha addressed. One can imagine his using verses like 13–14 to explain the real causes of a village quarrel, or even of a war. Everyone would have known that a poorly thatched roof will leak during the monsoon rains. Now they could understand how conflicts arise when hostile thoughts leak into an untrained mind.

To the Buddha, of course, training the mind meant meditation: the regular discipline of concentrating the mind and

making it one-pointed at will. Even in the Dhammapada –
that is, even for his lay followers – the Buddha emphasizes the
practice of meditation above all else. But meditation is a ter-
ribly difficult discipline. Why did the Buddha take such pains
to communicate his lofty meaning to masses of people who
would probably never have time or means to practice meditation? The answer is that the Buddha was an incorrigible opti-
mist. "I am confident," he once said, "confident with the highest of confidence." When writers call him a "spiritual demo-
crat," they mean he felt sure he could go anywhere in India and
find that needle in the haystack, the person who would come
up after the sermon and say, "I want to know more about how
to prevent hostile thoughts from arising. Please teach me."
The serious student is what every teacher seeks, and the Buddha found enough of them in these crowds to build a movement that has had a powerful and enduring effect on people's
hearts and lives for centuries.

– S.R.

1 ❏: *Twin Verses*

¹ All that we are is the result of what we have thought: we are formed and molded by our thoughts. Those whose minds are shaped by selfish thoughts cause misery when they speak or act. Sorrows roll over them as the wheels of a cart roll over the tracks of the bullock that draws it.

² All that we are is the result of what we have thought: we are formed and molded by our thoughts. Those whose minds are shaped by selfless thoughts give joy whenever they speak or act. Joy follows them like a shadow that never leaves them.

³ "He insulted me, he struck me, he cheated me, he robbed me": those caught in resentful thoughts never find peace.

CHAPTER ONE

⁴ "He insulted me, he struck me, he cheated
me, he robbed me": those who give up
resentful thoughts surely find peace.

⁵ For hatred does not cease by hatred at any time:
hatred ceases by love. This is an unalterable law.

⁶ There are those who forget that death will come
to all. For those who remember, quarrels come to
an end.

⁷ Those who live only for pleasure, who eat
intemperately, who are lazy and weak and lack
control over their senses, are like a tree with shallow
roots. As a strong wind uproots such a tree, Mara
the Tempter will throw such a person down. ⁸ But
those who live without looking for pleasure, who
eat temperately and control their senses, who are
persevering and firm in faith, are like a mountain.
As a strong wind cannot uproot a mountain,
Mara cannot throw such a person down.

⁹ Whoever puts on the saffron robe but is self-
willed, speaks untruthfully, and lacks self-
control is not worthy of that sacred garment.

¹⁰But those who have vanquished self-will,
who speak the truth and have mastered
themselves, are firmly established on the
spiritual path and worthy of the saffron robe.

¹¹The deluded, imagining trivial things to be vital
to life, follow their vain fancies and never attain the
highest knowledge. ¹²But the wise, knowing what
is trivial and what is vital, set their thoughts on the
supreme goal and attain the highest knowledge.

¹³As rain seeps through a poorly thatched roof,
passion seeps into the untrained mind.
¹⁴As rain cannot seep through a well-thatched roof,
passion cannot seep into a well-trained mind.

¹⁵Those who are selfish suffer here and suffer
there; they suffer wherever they go. They suffer
and fret over the damage they have done. ¹⁶But
those who are selfless rejoice here and rejoice
there; they rejoice wherever they go. They rejoice
and delight in the good they have done.

¹⁷The selfish person suffers here, and he suffers
there; he suffers wherever he goes. He suffers as he
broods over the damage he has done. He suffers more
and more as he travels along the path of sorrow.

¹⁸The selfless person is happy here, and he is happy there; he is happy wherever he goes. He is happy when he thinks of the good he has done. He grows in happiness as he progresses along the path of bliss.

¹⁹Those who recite many scriptures but do not practice their teachings are like a cowherd counting another's cows. They do not share in the joys of the spiritual life. ²⁰ But those who may know few scriptures but practice their teachings, who overcome all lust, hatred, and delusion, live with a pure mind in the highest wisdom. They stand without external supports and share in the joys of the spiritual life.

2 II: *Vigilance*

[21] Be vigilant and go beyond death. If you lack
vigilance, you cannot escape death. Those who
strive earnestly will go beyond death; those who do
not can never come to life. [22] The wise understand
this, and rejoice in the wisdom of the noble ones.
[23] Meditating earnestly and striving for nirvana,
they attain the highest joy and freedom.

[24] If you meditate earnestly, pure in mind and kind
in deeds, leading a disciplined life in harmony with
the dharma, you will grow in glory. [25] If you meditate
earnestly, through spiritual disciplines you can make
an island for yourself that no flood can overwhelm.

[26] The immature lose their vigilance, but the wise
guard it as their greatest treasure. [27] Do not fall
into ways of sloth and lust. Those who meditate
earnestly attain the highest happiness.

²⁸ Overcoming sloth through earnestness, the wise climb beyond suffering to the peaks of wisdom. They look upon the suffering multitude as one from a mountaintop looks on the plains below.

²⁹ Earnest among those who are indolent, awake among those who slumber, the wise advance like a racehorse, leaving others behind. ³⁰ It was through earnest effort that Indra became lord of the gods. The earnest are always respected, the indolent never.

³¹ The earnest spiritual aspirant, fearing sloth, advances like a fire, burning all fetters. ³² Such seekers will never fall back: they are nearing nirvana.

❶ *Mind & Flowers*

CONTROL OF THE MIND, the theme of chapter 3, is the most challenging and the most rewarding of human tasks, and the Buddha does not underestimate its difficulties. The mind, he suggests, has a depth far greater than the deepest sea, and all the way down it churns with emotional tempests of which we are barely conscious, but which virtually dictate thought and behavior.

According to the Buddha, we don't need any hell or afterlife to look for the devil. The mind itself – quick, fickle, and exceedingly difficult to focus – is the realm of Mara (34). In its depths lie untapped sources of great power: desires and drives of such magnitude that the mind is rarely under any real control; it simply moves about as it likes (35). To train these forces to obey the conscious will, the Buddha says, is the only way to be free from the mind's race-old urges and proddings. But this kind of training, Mahatma Gandhi once said, requires the patience of someone trying to empty the sea with a teacup.

The method for training the mind is meditation. One way

to visualize what happens in meditation is to think of the raw stuff of consciousness as clay, shaped on the potter's wheel of the mind. The shapes this clay has taken – strong desires, fears, attitudes, and aspirations, every habitual way of thinking – determine a person's behavior. Meditation slowly allows access to a level of awareness where these rigid shapes can be softened and made pliable again, until finally consciousness becomes like amorphous clay. Then the mind has no habits. It rests in its native state – calm, clear, adaptable, and endlessly responsive. Action then is no longer a matter of stimulus and response; it becomes unconditioned, spontaneous, and free.

This achievement is exceedingly difficult, however, because the mind churns with distracting thoughts that prevent us from going deep enough in meditation to make the necessary changes. However one tries to concentrate, the mind has subtle ways of wandering away to some desire or activity over which we have little conscious control. It is hard to imagine a more apt simile than verse 34, where the mind is compared to a fish out of water, gasping and thrashing about.

One who has truly learned to meditate, the Buddha says, can aim thoughts with the accuracy and power of a skilled archer (33); instead of thoughts going in all directions, each one finds its mark. These martial associations are appropriate, for meditation is a battle and this arrow is "the weapon of wisdom" (40). No conqueror, not even Napoleon or Alexander, ever fought a battle more significant than that waged for control over one's own mind. To win, the Buddha says in a later verse (103), is a greater feat than conquering a thousand times a thousand men on the battlefield. It means, ultimately, the conquest of death itself (21), an achievement no worldly conqueror can claim.

Until this victory is gained, however, the mind is still out of control; and an undisciplined mind not only cannot be relied on, it cannot avoid doing harm. Verse 41 provides a grim glimpse of the inevitable fate of those who fail to train the mind. This is an example of what Buddhists call a meditation on bodily decay – a device used in monastic circles to resist the powerful physical passions and longings that assault a person trying to master the mind. Monastics may have pursued this grim line a little more vigorously than the Buddha recommended on what he called the Middle Path. Nevertheless, it can surely be said that nothing caused him more grief than the human being's shortsighted pursuit of satisfactions that cannot last. That is why he so pressingly urged everyone to shun ephemeral activities in order to pursue the only accomplishment that lasts. In the Sutta Nipata (1092–94) a youth named Kappa asks: "Tell me about an island where all this suffering will be no more." And the Buddha replies:

Kappa, for those struggling in midstream, in great fear of
the flood, of growing old and of dying – for all those I say,

an island exists where there is no place for impediments, no place for clinging: the island of no going beyond. I call it nirvana, the complete destruction of old age and dying.

It may seem surprising that the Buddha devotes so much attention to suspending the operations of that very instrument which people associate with human progress. All of the major material accomplishments of our civilization – the development of the machine, the conquest of disease, the triumph of technology – stem from creative thought. However, no one today would claim that such exploits have taken humanity beyond suffering, much less that they can free a person from death: both of which, the Buddha claims, come when the mind is stilled.

Moreover, less laudable feats – the poisoning of the environment, the production of weapons powerful enough to destroy all of life – also can be traced to creative thought. So long as the mind is not under control, the Buddha says, destructive thoughts cannot be kept out, and selfish motives cannot help bringing undesirable results as well as desirable ones. The inertial drift of millions of such minds, not evil but simply uncontrolled, can take the world to a precipice. Yet as the Buddha implies in a later verse, the power of a well-trained mind is such that one clearheaded, compassionate individual, appealing deeply to what is best in human nature, can be enough to reverse a destructive course of action.

– S.R.

3 ❚ *Mind*

³³ As an archer aims an arrow, the wise aim their
restless thoughts, hard to aim, hard to restrain.

³⁴ As a fish hooked and left on the sand thrashes
about in agony, the mind being trained in meditation
trembles all over, desperate to escape the hand of
Mara.

³⁵ Hard it is to train the mind, which goes where it
likes and does what it wants. But a trained mind
brings health and happiness. ³⁶ The wise can direct
their thoughts, subtle and elusive, wherever they
choose: a trained mind brings health and happiness.

³⁷ Those who can direct thoughts, which are
unsubstantial and wander so aimlessly, are freed
from the bonds of Mara.

³⁸ They are not wise whose thoughts are not steady
and minds not serene, who do not know dharma,

the law of life. ³⁹ They are wise whose thoughts
are steady and minds serene, unaffected by good
and bad. They are awake and free from fear.

⁴⁰ Remember, this body is like a fragile clay pot.
Make your mind a fortress and conquer Mara with
the weapon of wisdom. Guard your conquest always.
⁴¹ Remember that this body will soon lie in the earth
without life, without value, useless as a burned log.

⁴² More than those who hate you, more than
all your enemies, an undisciplined mind does
greater harm. ⁴³ More than your mother, more
than your father, more than all your family, a
well-disciplined mind does greater good.

4 ▫ *Flowers*

⁴⁴ As a garland-maker chooses the right flowers,
choose the well-taught path of dharma and go
beyond the realms of death and of the gods. ⁴⁵ As
a garland-maker chooses the right flowers, those
who choose the well-taught path of dharma will
go beyond the realms of death and of the gods.

⁴⁶ Remembering that this body is like froth, of the
nature of a mirage, break the flower-tipped arrows
of Mara. Never again will death touch you.

⁴⁷ As a flood sweeps away a slumbering village, death
sweeps away those who spend their lives gathering
flowers. ⁴⁸ Death sweeps them away while they are
still gathering, caught in the pursuit of pleasure.
⁴⁹ But the wise live without injuring nature, as the
bee drinks nectar without harming the flower.

CHAPTER FOUR

50 Do not give your attention to what others do
or fail to do; give it to what you do or fail to do.

51 Like a lovely flower, full of color but lacking
in fragrance, are the words of those who do
not practice what they preach. **52** Like a lovely
flower full of color and fragrance are the words
of those who practice what they preach.

53 Many garlands can be made from a heap of
flowers. Many good deeds can be done in this life.

54 The scent of flowers or sandalwood cannot
travel against the wind; but the fragrance of the
good spreads everywhere. **55** Neither sandalwood
nor the *tagara* flower, neither lotus nor jasmine,
can come near the fragrance of the good.

56 Faint is the scent of sandalwood or the *tagara*,
but the fragrance of the good rises high to reach
the gods. **57** Mara can never come near those
who are good, earnest, and enlightened.

58-59 A true follower of the Buddha shines among
blind mortals as the fragrant lotus, growing in the
garbage by the roadside, brings joy to all who pass by.

◻: *The Immature & The Wise*

THE TITLE OF chapter 5 is usually translated as "The Fool" and that of chapter 6 as "The Wise," as if they dealt with utterly opposite temperaments. However, *bala* means not only "fool" but "child." A fool's behavior is not likely to improve, but a child is simply immature; given time and experience, children grow up. The Buddha was a compassionate teacher whose path was open to people of all capacities; he would not deprecate anyone's ability to grow. Translating *bala* as "immature" gives all of us the benefit of the doubt, as the Buddha always did.

But the Buddha was also a realist, and these verses show it. In the Anguttara Nikaya (1.59) he defines the immature person succinctly:

> Monks, there are two kinds of immature people: those who do not see their own mistakes as mistakes, and those who do not forgive mistakes committed by someone else.

The evolution from immaturity to wisdom is a long road, longest of all for those who do not base their actions on some deeper purpose in life. The word *samsara* in verse 60, which refers to the cycle of birth and death, means literally "that which is moving intensely," that is, the everyday world of incessant change. Immature people, living unreflectively from moment to moment, drown in the instability of samsara, which drags on as endlessly as night for the insomniac. That is because this kind of immaturity is not that of a child, but of the adult who is not sensitive to that moment of discrimination when one choice will lead toward wisdom and the other to bitter pain (66). Lacking that sensitivity, he has to undergo a good deal of pain to learn from life, for even the bitterest suffering does not carry his understanding very far forward. Like a spoon that cannot savor the taste of soup, he is impervious to wisdom even when it is in the very air around him (64).

Yet an immature person can always learn to grow. Knowledge itself cannot lead such people to wisdom because, lacking sound discrimination, they will misuse it so badly that they will "break their heads" against it (72). But if those who are immature have enough self-knowledge to realize that they are immature, that is the beginning of wisdom (63); it will save them from having to undergo the painful experience that many unwise actions would otherwise have inflicted on them.

One of the main distinctions between immaturity and wisdom lies in one's ability to assimilate teaching. The immature person was compared to a spoon in soup; the wise can taste the soup and savor the subtleties of its flavor (65). Instead of being victimized by experience, they make conscious use of it to remove undesirable traits, reshaping their character as a carpenter shapes a piece of wood (80). While the immature look for opportunities to gain praise, the wise seek out someone who will help them "reveal hidden treasures" (76), even though such a person might well criticize their weaknesses or keep them from doing something which, though pleasant, will only prove injurious. The role of the teacher in this process is simply that of a wise advisor. The Buddha teaches us to rely on ourselves to do what is necessary to gain the goal. "All the effort must be made by you," he says in a later verse (276). "Buddhas only show the way."

Verse 89 mentions the "seven fields of enlightenment": mindfulness, vigor, joy, serenity, concentration, equanimity, and "penetration of dharma" – that is, seeing the workings of dharma everywhere, even in the events of everyday life. In Buddhism, enlightenment (*sambodhi* or *bodhi*) is an instantaneous experience in which mental activity is momentarily suspended completely and sleeping realms of consciousness are dazzled into full wakefulness. Bodhi is not nirvana. It is a temporary stilling of the mind, which brings illumination of consciousness; nirvana, the permanent release from all sources of suffering, is attained only when the experience of enlightenment has been repeated so often that it, not ordinary conditioned awareness, has become one's constant state. Only when the insights of bodhi are completely absorbed into one's character and conduct would the Buddha call a person truly awake.

– S.R.

5 ∎ *The Immature*

⁶⁰ Long is the night to those who are awake; long is the road to those who are weary. Long is the cycle of birth and death to those who know not the dharma.

⁶¹ If you find no one to support you on the spiritual path, walk alone. There is no companionship with the immature. ⁶² They think, "These children are mine; this wealth is mine." They cannot even call themselves their own, much less their children or wealth.

⁶³ The immature who know they are immature have a little wisdom. But the immature who look on themselves as wise are utterly foolish. ⁶⁴ They cannot understand the dharma even if they spend their whole life with the wise. How can the spoon know the taste of soup? ⁶⁵ If the mature spend even a short time with the wise, they will understand dharma, just as the tongue knows the taste of soup.

CHAPTER FIVE

⁶⁶ The immature are their own enemies, doing selfish deeds which will bring them sorrow. ⁶⁷ That deed is selfish which brings remorse and suffering in its wake. ⁶⁸ But good is that deed which brings no remorse, only happiness in its wake.

⁶⁹ Sweet are selfish deeds to the immature until they see the results; when they see the results, they suffer. ⁷⁰ Even if they fast month after month, eating with only the tip of a blade of grass, they are not worth a sixteenth part of one who truly understands dharma.

⁷¹ As fresh milk needs time to curdle, a selfish deed takes time to bring sorrow in its wake. Like fire smoldering under the ashes, slowly does it burn the immature.

⁷² Even if they pick up a little knowledge, the immature misuse it and break their heads instead of benefiting from it.

⁷³ The immature go after false prestige – precedence of fellow monks, power in the monasteries, and praise from all. ⁷⁴ "Listen, monks and householders, I can do this; I can do that. I am right and you are wrong." Thus their pride and passion increase.

[75] Choose the path that leads to nirvana; avoid the road to profit and pleasure. Remember this always, O disciples of the Buddha, and strive always for wisdom.

6 ▯ *The Wise*

⁷⁶ If you see someone wise, who can steer you away from the wrong path, follow that person as you would one who can reveal hidden treasures. Only good can come out of it.

⁷⁷ Let them admonish or instruct or restrain you from what is wrong. They will be loved by the good but disliked by the bad.

⁷⁸ Make friends with those who are good and true, not with those who are bad and false.

⁷⁹ To follow the dharma revealed by the noble ones is to live in joy with a serene mind.

⁸⁰ As irrigators lead water where they want, as archers make their arrows straight, as carpenters carve wood, the wise shape their minds.

81 As a solid rock cannot be moved by the wind, the
wise are not shaken by praise or blame. **82** When
they listen to the words of the dharma, their minds
become calm and clear like the waters of a still lake.

83 Good people keep on walking whatever happens.
They do not speak vain words and are the same in
good fortune and bad. **84** If one desires neither children
nor wealth nor power nor success by unfair means,
know such a one to be good, wise, and virtuous.

85 Few are those who reach the other shore; most
people keep running up and down this shore.
86 But those who follow the dharma, when it
has been well taught, will reach the other shore,
hard to reach, beyond the power of death.

87-88 They leave darkness behind and follow the
light. They give up home and leave pleasure behind.
Calling nothing their own, they purify their hearts
and rejoice. **89** Well trained in the seven fields of
enlightenment, their senses disciplined and free from
attachments, they live in freedom, full of light.

❐: *The Saint & Thousands*

CHAPTER 6 DEALT with the man or woman steadily increasing in wisdom; chapter 7 treats the person who is completely illumined: *arhant*, literally "one who is deserving." An arhant is that person who, having developed the fullness of humanity by attaining nirvana, now truly deserves to be called a human being.

If life is conceived of as a school where all are training for full spiritual development, the arhant is the graduate. "Profound, measureless, unfathomable is the arhant, like the great ocean," says the Buddha. "The concept 'reborn' does not apply to such a person, nor 'not reborn,' nor any combination of such words." Dozens of monks, nuns, and lay followers are said to have attained this state within the Buddha's lifetime.

Arhantship is the goal of the spiritual journey, fourth and last of the phases passed through in the course of attaining full realization of the Buddhist ideal. In the first of these phases the aspirant is called a "stream-winner" (*srotapanna*). While the immature are said to run up and down this shore of sorrow, making no intentional use of their experience to further spiritual growth, the "stream-winner" has begun to practice the Eightfold Path; such people have plunged into the stream that leads to nirvana. Their direction is not with the current but upstream, against all the normal urges of human conditioning.

After a good deal of arduous effort, generally over many lives, the aspirant becomes a "once-returner" (*sakridagamin*), one who has sighted the other shore of nirvana but not yet reached it. For such a person, the crossing can be completed in just one more life.

Those who finally reach the other shore become a "never-returner" (*anagamin*). Their purpose in life is fulfilled, and therefore they need never be born again. They may then become an *arhant* – one whose path in life cannot even be traced (92–93) because their actions no longer leave behind the residue of karma. Their responses to life are not dictated by what happens to them, whether good or bad; they act in complete freedom. The cycle of birth and death no longer contains them (95). Since they lack nothing, there is nothing that life has to offer that they need or desire.

Yet the Buddha would still prod such people to make their fullest contribution to others. He said to his disciples:

> Go forth, therefore, brethren, on your journey, for the joy of the many, for the happiness of the many, out of compassion for the world. Teach the dharma which is beautiful at the

beginning, beautiful in the middle, and beautiful at the end. Let not any two of you go together. (Vinaya Pitaka 1.20–21)

Despite such statements, some maintain that the arhant ideal, full freedom from the cycle of birth and death, is not the highest. Mahayana Buddhists went so far as to call the arhant a "private Buddha" (*pratyeka-buddha*), implying that such people do not share the fruits of their attainment, deserting a suffering humanity to bask in nirvana. The Mahayana ideal was called *bodhisattva*, literally "one whose nature is enlightenment." In early Buddhism, as in the present-day Theravada tradition, the word *bodhisattva* referred solely to that being who, before becoming the Buddha, had vowed to become a Buddha over many lives in the distant past, and who finally attained nirvana in his life as Prince Siddhartha. To the later Mahayanists, *bodhisattva* came to mean anyone who vows to be reborn countless times, never to enter final nirvana until the last sentient being is rescued from samsara.

Because of the divergence of the Mahayana and Theravada schools, the ideals of arhant and bodhisattva are commonly contrasted, and from a philosophical standpoint they seem very different. The arhant has won permanent release from samsara, while the bodhisattva chooses to return to it until the very end of time. The distinction, however, may be of no more than philosophical interest. To someone actually trying to practice the Buddha's disciplines, the arhant has the same inestimable value as the bodhisattva in terms of what they give to the rest of life. Both supply us with the loftiest possible image of the human being; both are living embodiments of that goal toward which all humanity blindly gropes. When the brahmin Sangarava criticized the Buddha for the supposed selfishness of his spiritual ideal, the Buddha traced out the career of an enlightened person and let the brahmin draw his own conclusions. A Buddha, he explained,

> speaks like this: "Come, this is the Way, the practice which I have followed. Having fully mastered it, and having by my own powers of knowing plunged into the incomparable bliss of the spiritual life, I have told that Way to others. Come and follow likewise, so that you too, having mastered the practice and, by your own powers of knowing, plunged into the incomparable bliss of the spiritual life, may abide in it." In this way the teacher teaches dharma, and others follow to attain that goal. Such teachers, moreover, number many hundreds, many thousands, many hundreds of thousands. If this be the case, do you think the merit of having taken to the spiritual life benefits just one person or many? (Anguttara Nikaya 1.167–168)

In a world whose survival is in doubt from day to day, those who have conquered the passions that wreck relationships and precipitate wars serve their fellow creatures ceaselessly in a way that no one else can, and in a way that will not end with death. That fact transcends any philosophical difference between the arhant and the bodhisattva.

—S.R.

7 ॥ *The Saint*

⁹⁰ They have completed their voyage; they have
gone beyond sorrow. The fetters of life have fallen
from them, and they live in full freedom.

⁹¹ The thoughtful strive always. They have no fixed
abode, but leave home like swans from their lake.

⁹² Like the flight of birds in the sky, the path of the
selfless is hard to follow. They have no possessions,
but live on alms in a world of freedom. ⁹³ Like
the flight of birds in the sky, their path is hard to
follow. With their senses under control, temperate
in eating, they know the meaning of freedom.

⁹⁴ Even the gods envy the saints, whose senses
obey them like well-trained horses and who are
free from pride. ⁹⁵ Patient like the earth, they stand
like a threshold. They are pure like a lake without
mud, and free from the cycle of birth and death.

CHAPTER SEVEN

⁹⁶ Wisdom has stilled their minds, and their
thoughts, words, and deeds are filled with peace.
⁹⁷ Freed from illusion and from personal ties, they
have renounced the world of appearance to find
reality. Thus have they reached the highest.

⁹⁸ They make holy wherever they dwell, in village or
forest, on land or at sea. ⁹⁹ With their senses at peace
and minds full of joy, they make the forests holy.

8 ◦ *Thousands*

¹⁰⁰ Better than a speech of a thousand vain words is
one thoughtful word which brings peace to the mind.
¹⁰¹ Better than a poem of a thousand vain verses is
one thoughtful line which brings peace to the mind.
¹⁰² Better than a hundred poems of vain stanzas is one
word of the dharma that brings peace to the mind.

¹⁰³ One who conquers himself is greater than another
who conquers a thousand times a thousand men
on the battlefield. ^{104–105} Be victorious over yourself
and not over others. When you attain victory over
yourself, not even the gods can turn it into defeat.

¹⁰⁶ Better than performing a thousand rituals month
by month for a hundred years is a moment's homage
to one living in wisdom. ¹⁰⁷ Better than tending the
sacrificial fire in the forest for a thousand years is
a moment's homage to one living in wisdom.

CHAPTER EIGHT

[108] Making gifts and offerings for a whole year to
earn merit is not worth a quarter of the honor
paid to the wise. [109] To those who honor the wise
and follow them, four gifts will come in increasing
measure: health, happiness, beauty, and long life.

[110] Better to live in virtue and wisdom for one
day than to live a hundred years with an evil and
undisciplined mind. [111] Better to live in goodness
and wisdom for one day than to lead an ignorant and
undisciplined life for a hundred years. [112] Better to
live in strength and wisdom for one day than to lead
a weak and idle life for a hundred years. [113] Better to
live in freedom and wisdom for one day than to lead
a conditioned life of bondage for a hundred years.

[114] One day's glimpse of the deathless state is
better than a hundred years of life without
it. [115] One day's glimpse of dharma is better
than a hundred years of life without it.

CHAPTERS NINE & TEN

▯⦂ Evil & Punishment

WRONG ACTIONS ARE central to the concept of *papa*, "sin" or "evil," which is the theme of chapter 9 and continues on into chapter 10. In Buddhism there is no one sitting in judgment to punish us for wrong actions, nor is there anyone to reward us for our good works. Instead, reward and punishment issue from the self-fulfilling law of karma, which permeates every aspect of the Buddha's teachings. Put simply, the law of karma states that as we sow, so shall we reap: everything we do, say, or even think has consequences, good or bad, and sooner or later those consequences must come back to us. Karma was already an ancient idea in India when the Buddha taught, and it can safely be said that his audience took for granted that the law of cause and effect governs not only physical events, but every event in human experience.

Like any physical law, the law of karma operates everywhere and at every moment. It is totally impersonal, requiring no agency other than ourselves. The Buddha taught that for an action to produce karma, it has to be accompanied by a conscious will, which presupposes the capacity of free choice. If a small child hits another child, there is probably no karmic residue, because he is still innocent and does not fully acquiesce in the action as an adult would have to; he may be playing happily with the same child minutes later. But when an adult says angry words to someone, the will is an accomplice, and the action will bear fruit (136). It is impossible to escape the karmic result of action no matter where we may try (127). The karma must return in kind, whether good or bad, even though it may take time for the right circumstances to come around (119–120).

According to the Buddha, a large part of our experience is simply the mechanical return of the karma our previous actions have accumulated. "Previous actions" here, of course, extends to previous lives. These ideas too were an integral part of the Buddha's Hindu background, but no one else in Indian mysticism worked out their significance with greater breadth and precision. Dharma is a seamless web in which physical and mental events are inescapably intertwined, and even disasters or misfortunes may be a delayed karmic reaction to something we did in this life or in some previous life (137–140).

One aspect of the law of karma receives special attention in this chapter: that is the concept of *samskaras*, or karma-formed states. A samskara involves not just one action and its karmic return, but a mental inclination to act in a certain way. The reason the Buddha cautions us against repeating wrong actions – and recommends repeating good actions (117–118) – is that such habits cut a track in consciousness upon which future actions in similar circumstances are likely to run.

If we continue to commit a mistake – say, an outburst of anger – each repetition makes it easier to make the same mistake again, so that gradually anger becomes part of our character. That is very close to what the Buddha means by a samskara: a habit of thinking which karmically locks us into patterns of behavior over which we have less and less control with every succeeding repetition. In a samskara like anger, karma acts on the individual not just in his external environment, but also from within. An anger-prone person may get anger returned to him from other individuals, but he may also suffer karmic harm within: increased anxiety, risk of heart disease or other behavior-aggravated ailments, the turmoil of an unruly mind.

Because it is easiest to follow the worn path of stimulus and response, harmful samskaras are easy to form and to get trapped in. Actively asserting the responses that do *not* come naturally – forgiveness, patience, compassion in the face of hatred – is the only way to avoid gradually succumbing to evil (116): that is, to avoid becoming internally laced with harmful samskaras. In a very real way, we are what our samskaras are: as the network of choice-pathways in us, they constitute the karmic legacy of all our previous choices. Evil in Buddhism thus becomes a question of rightly understanding how a person becomes prone to harmful action and what courses of action can set the situation right.

The Buddha's emphasis is always on choice, and his prognosis is always hopeful. He shows us the power of evil habits, then reminds us that good habits are just as strong (121–122). If we do not try to shape our lives, the conditioning of our samskaras will shape them for us, little by little; but if we do try – again, little by little, in the numberless decisions of everyday life – then any one of us can become good, as a bucket is filled drop by drop.

—S.R.

9 ॥ *Evil*

¹¹⁶ Hasten to do good; refrain from evil. If you
neglect the good, evil can enter your mind.

¹¹⁷ If you do what is evil, do not repeat it or take
pleasure in making it a habit. An evil habit will cause
nothing but suffering. ¹¹⁸ If you do what is good,
keep repeating it and take pleasure in making it a
habit. A good habit will cause nothing but joy.

¹¹⁹ Evildoers may be happy as long as they do
not reap what they have sown, but when they
do, sorrow overcomes them. ¹²⁰ The good may
suffer as long as they do not reap what they have
sown, but when they do, joy overcomes them.

¹²¹ Let no one think lightly of evil and say to himself,
"Sorrow will not come to me." Little by little a person
becomes evil, as a pot is filled by drops of water.

CHAPTER NINE

¹²²Let no one think lightly of good and say to himself, "Joy will not come to me." Little by little a person becomes good, as a pot is filled by drops of water.

¹²³ As a rich merchant traveling alone avoids dangerous roads, as a lover of life avoids poison, let everyone avoid dangerous deeds.

¹²⁴ If you have no wound on your hand, you can touch poison without being harmed. No harm comes to those who do no harm. ¹²⁵ If you harm a pure and innocent person, you harm yourself, as dust thrown against the wind comes back to the thrower.

¹²⁶ Some are born again. Those caught in evil ways go to a state of intense suffering; those who have done good go to a state of joy. But the pure in heart enter nirvana.

¹²⁷ Not in the sky, not in the ocean, not in mountain canyons is there a place anywhere in the world where a person can hide from his evil deeds. ¹²⁸ Not in the sky, not in the ocean, not in mountain canyons is there a place where one can hide from death.

10 ▯: *Punishment*

¹²⁹ Everyone fears punishment; everyone fears death,
just as you do. Therefore do not kill or cause to kill.
¹³⁰ Everyone fears punishment; everyone loves life,
as you do. Therefore do not kill or cause to kill.

¹³¹ If, hoping to be happy, you strike at others who
also seek happiness, you will be happy neither
here nor hereafter. ¹³² If, hoping to be happy,
you do not strike at others who are also seeking
happiness, you will be happy here and hereafter.

¹³³ Speak quietly to everyone, and they too will
be gentle in their speech. Harsh words hurt,
and come back to the speaker. ¹³⁴ If your mind
is still, like a broken gong, you have entered
nirvana, leaving all quarrels behind you.

CHAPTER TEN

[135] As a cowherd with his staff drives cows to fresh fields, old age and death lead all creatures to new lives. [136] The selfish, doing harm, do not know what is in store for them. They are burned as if by fire by the results of their own deeds.

[137] If one harms the innocent, suffering will come in these ten ways. [138] They may suffer grief, infirmity, painful accident, serious illness, [139] loss of mind, legal prosecution, fearful accusation, family bereavement, or financial loss; [140] or their house may burn down, and after death they may be thrown into the fire of suffering.

[141] Going about with matted hair, without food or bath, sleeping on the ground smeared with dust or sitting motionless – no amount of penance can help a person whose mind is not purified. [142] But those whose mind is serene and chaste, whose senses are controlled and whose life is nonviolent – these are true brahmins, true monks, even if they wear fine clothes.

[143] As a well-trained horse needs no whip, a well-trained mind needs no prodding from the world to be good. [144] Be like a well-trained horse, swift

and spirited, and go beyond sorrow through faith,
meditation, and energetic practice of the dharma.

145 As irrigators guide water to their fields,
as archers aim arrows, as carpenters carve
wood, the wise shape their lives.

CHAPTER ELEVEN

⫶ *Age*

JARA, "OLD AGE," is a Sanskrit word
originally applied to a worn-out, dilapidated building. The
second Noble Sight that led Prince Siddhartha to renounce
worldly life and seek nirvana was of an ancient, disfigured
man barely able to walk. The sight plunged him deep into consciousness to confront the decay for which every body is des-
tined. Few people look forward to the onset of wrinkles and
stiff joints, but only a spiritual genius confronts the full meaning of old age all at once, seeing age as a process that begins
the moment we are conceived. This chapter begins on a sober
note, with a plea that all take note of the fire of advancing age
rather than lightly making merry (146).

Many of the verses in this chapter are meant to instill a fear
that old age will overtake us before we have realized our real
purpose, making life a tragic waste. Yet it would be a mistake to conclude that the Buddha's message was life-denying,
or conclude from verses 147–148 that he viewed the human
body with distaste. He has the greatest respect for the human

body, and in fact maintained that human birth is the highest
of blessings because it is only as human beings that we can
strive for and attain nirvana. These verses are simply meant
to communicate what little value he sees in a purely physical existence, spending our time on pleasing the body and
senses instead of using each day of an all-too-short life to take
another step toward the goal.

The view of the Buddha on this subject is glimpsed in
verses 153–154, perhaps better than anywhere else in Buddhist
literature. These are the celebrated "housebuilder verses,"
said to have been uttered by the Buddha immediately after
his enlightenment under the bodhi tree: the paean of joy that
issues from his lips when he realizes that life's goal is won.
After wandering in samsara life after life, he has finally come
face to face with selfish craving, the architect of separate existence, and put an end to it once and for all.

In Hindu and Buddhist psychology, craving is a force
which keeps seeking physical embodiment – another birth –
for the satisfaction of physical desires. Yet the physical body
cannot help aging, becoming less and less able to deliver satisfaction; and the less it can please, the more insistent craving
becomes. The Sanskrit poet Bhartrihari captures this process
in his "Century of Verses on Renunciation":

> My face is overrun with wrinkles,
> My head is marked with gray.

My limbs have gone flaccid;
Craving alone keeps its youth and vigor.

(Vairagya Shataka 156)

Each life not spent in reducing selfish craving, therefore, impels a person into the next life with cravings that are fiercer than ever. It is in this sense that selfish craving is the architect of body and personality, and that its extinction brings freedom from all selfish conditioning.

The Buddha expresses enlightenment not as a meeting with God or an immersion in bliss, but as the disassembling of the conditioned personality and the exhilaration that comes with perfect freedom. Through his own effort he has undone the force that has conditioned his entire making, from the smallest unicellular organism at the dawn of evolution to the wonder of the individual that was Prince Siddhartha. Bursting through to the Unconditioned, he has destroyed craving; never again can he be compelled by karma to return to life as a separate creature.

−S.R.

11 ॥ *Age*

146 Why is there laughter, why merriment, when
this world is on fire? When you are living in
darkness, why don't you look for light?

147-148 This body is a painted image, subject
to disease, decay and death, held together by
thoughts that come and go. **149** What joy can
there be for those who see that their white bones
will be cast away like gourds in the autumn?

150 Around the bones is built a house, plastered
with flesh and blood, in which dwell pride and
pretence, old age and death. **151** Even the chariot of
a king loses its glitter in the course of time; so too
the body loses its health and strength. But goodness
does not grow old with the passage of time.

¹⁵² A man who does not learn from life grows old like an ox: his body grows, but not his wisdom.

¹⁵³ I have gone through many rounds of birth and death, looking in vain for the builder of this body. Heavy indeed is birth and death again and again! ¹⁵⁴ But now I have seen you, housebuilder; you shall not build this house again. Its beams are broken; its dome is shattered: self-will is extinguished; nirvana is attained.

¹⁵⁵ Those who have not practiced spiritual disciplines in their youth pine away like old cranes in a lake without fish. ¹⁵⁶ Like worn-out bows they lie in old age, sighing over the past.

CHAPTER TWELVE
▯: *Self*

ATMAN OR "SELF," the subject of this chapter, has stirred more controversy than any other subject in the Buddha's teachings. Several times throughout the Pali canon the Buddha says that the human being is *anatman*, "without a self," thus apparently contradicting a principle that is the very basis of the Hindu faith: that at the core of every creature is a divine Self (*Atman*) which is not different from the transcendent reality (*Brahman*) and is therefore utterly beyond the world of change and death. Discussing how a transcendent Self can relate to an impermanent personality naturally plunged Indian philosophers into deep metaphysical waters. But the Buddha never indulged in metaphysics. His concern was relentlessly practical: life is full of suffering, the cause of that suffering is selfishness, and selfishness can be removed by practicing the Eightfold Path. Anything else is a distraction. On what lay beyond the impermanent world of ego and change, his attitude was simply, "First go there; then you will see for yourself."

On one occasion, a monk asked the Buddha if belief in a permanent Self can prove harmful. The Buddha replied that it can. "Suppose," he explained,

> that a man has the following view: "The universe is that Self, and I shall be that after death: permanent, abiding, everlasting, unchanging. I shall exist as that for eternity." Then he hears the Tathagata [the Buddha] or a disciple preaching that dharma which aims at the destruction of all views . . . at the extinction of craving, at detachment, at stopping, at nirvana. Then that man thinks, "I will be annihilated, destroyed, and be no more!" So he mourns, laments, and weeps, beating his breast, and becomes confused. Thus, O monk, there is a possibility that one will become tormented when something permanent within oneself is not found.
>
> (*Majjhima Nikaya* 1.22)

Scholars and orthodox Buddhists alike have cited such instances as proof that the Buddha denied the existence of a permanent Self, beyond all change and unaffected by death. Others cite more affirmative statements to assert that the Buddha *did* believe in a Self: in this chapter of the Dhammapada, for example, he exhorts us to rely solely on our self and seek no other support. Part of the ambiguity lies in the language. Depending on the context, the Sanskrit word *atman* can mean self in the conventional sense of "myself" and "yourself," or it can refer to the transcendent Self of the Upanishads. Hundreds of books have debated which the Buddha was denying, self or Self, so that many maintain his stand on self to be the most distinctive mark of his teaching.

It is, however, hard to imagine that the Buddha himself was interested in this controversy. His concern was in putting an end to self – that is, an end to ego. Nagarjuna, the brilliant Buddhist dialectician of the second century, claimed that self was used by the Buddha only as a teaching device and that he actually took no stand whatever on it:

> There is the teaching of Self
> And there is the teaching of not-Self.
> But by the Buddhas neither Self nor not-Self
> Has been taught as something that exists.
> (*Mulamadhyamika Karika* XVII.6)

He did not raise the question at all; it had no bearing on the actual practice of the Eightfold Path.

When the wanderer Vacchagotta came asking about the existence of the Self, for example, the Buddha would not even give him an answer. This occasion, called the Buddha's Noble Silence, contains his real answer to all metaphysical speculation. Though probably the most brilliant intellect of his time, the Buddha maintained no intellectual positions whatever. They would be counter to his only purpose, which was to inspire greater effort in spiritual practice. How can intellectual opinions about the unity of life help a person as long as he believes he is a separate ego? What difference does his opinion about eternity make as long as he is still caught up in time? By offering no metaphysical supports, the Buddha prompts us to plunge deep in meditation and see for ourselves what we discover. In this chapter, his emphasis is on putting forth utmost effort to develop self-reliance. In one of the most celebrated statements on this theme, he addresses these words to his disciple Ananda:

> Therefore, Ananda, live having self for an island, self for refuge and no other; having dharma for an island, dharma for refuge and no other.
>
> (*Samyutta Nikaya* v.162)

The self he speaks of in this passage and throughout this chapter is the human will, the only self worthy of strengthening and cultivation.

—S.R.

12 ◦ Self

¹⁵⁷ If you hold yourself dear, guard yourself diligently.
Keep vigil during one of the three watches of the night.

¹⁵⁸ Learn what is right; then teach others, as
the wise do. ¹⁵⁹ Before trying to guide others, be your
own guide first. It is hard to learn to guide oneself.

¹⁶⁰ Your own self is your master; who else could be?
With yourself well controlled, you gain a master very
hard to find.

¹⁶¹ The evil done by the selfish crushes them as a
diamond breaks a hard gem. ¹⁶² As a vine overpowers
a tree, evil overpowers those who do evil, trapping
them in a situation that only their enemies would
wish them to be in. ¹⁶³Evil deeds, which harm the
doer, are easy to do; good deeds are not so easy.

164 Foolish people who scoff at the teachings of
the wise, the noble, and the good, following false
doctrines, bring about their own downfall like the
khattaka tree, which dies after bearing fruit.

165 By oneself is evil done; by oneself one is
injured. Do not do evil, and suffering will
not come. Everyone has the choice to be pure
or impure. No one can purify another.

166 Don't neglect your own duty for another,
however great. Know your own duty and perform it.

⫶ *The World*

THE SUBJECT OF this chapter is *loka*, "the world": that environment into which we have been born. The Buddha compares this world to a royal chariot decked out in gaudy colors, all paint and show (171), which the wise know to be no more permanent than a bubble or a mirage. Unattached to its pleasures, they are detached too from its sufferings; thus they rise above its law of physical decay and death (170).

The Buddha speaks of states of consciousness as different worlds, all as real as everyday life to those having direct experience of them. Some of these are alluded to in this chapter: this world, the next world, the realm of the gods. But his primary distinction is between two essentially different levels of reality: *samvriti-satya*, "conventional reality" or the world of day-to-day life, and *paramartha-satya*, "absolute reality." The samvriti world has only a provisional reality because it is not the same from instant to instant; all of the experiences one has exist for a moment only, then vanish into nothingness.

But beneath this conventional level is a permanent ground of being: paramartha, which is completely unaffected by change. Samvriti is still real, but it has a lesser degree of reality, just as a dream experience belongs to a lower level of reality than the waking state.

In the everyday world, of course, the vast majority of us are unaware of a higher reality. Those few who have glimpsed it are compared by the Buddha to the fortunate birds who escape the hunter's net (174). The great ideal of Mahayana Buddhism is to remain in this world, so tempting and full of snares, but at the same time attain this awareness of the Absolute which underlies it, thus remaining free while helping others to free themselves. Nagarjuna captures the essence of this state when he proclaims,

> There is no difference at all between samsara and nirvana;
> There is no difference at all between samsara and nirvana.

—S.R.

13 ❧ *The World*

¹⁶⁷ Don't follow wrong laws; don't be
thoughtless; don't believe false doctrines.
Don't follow the way of the world.

¹⁶⁸⁻¹⁶⁹ Wake up! Don't be lazy. Follow the
right path, avoid the wrong. You will be
happy here as well as hereafter.

¹⁷⁰ Look on the world as a bubble; look on it
as a mirage. Then the King of Death cannot
even see you. ¹⁷¹Come look at this world! Is
it not like a painted royal chariot? The wise
see through it, but not the immature.

¹⁷² When those who are foolish become wise, they
give light to the world like the full moon breaking
through the clouds. ¹⁷³When their good deeds

overcome the bad, they give light to the world like the moon breaking free from behind the clouds.

174 In this dark world, few can see. Like birds that free themselves from the net, only a few find their way to heaven. 175Swans fly on the path of the sun by their wonderful power; the wise rise above the world, after conquering Mara and his train.

176 He who transgresses the central law of life, who speaks falsely or scoffs at the life to come, is capable of any evil.

177 Misers do not go to the world of the gods; they do not want to give. The wise are generous, and go to a happier world.

178 Better than ruling this world, better than attaining the realm of the gods, better than being lord of all the worlds, is one step taken on the path to nirvana.

CHAPTER FOURTEEN

◻: *The Awakened One*

"THE AWAKENED ONE," of course, is the literal meaning of the word *Buddha*, and most of the verses in this chapter describe the qualities cultivated and perfected by the Compassionate Buddha himself. But to understand verses like 184, where the Buddha calls patience a supreme spiritual discipline, it is helpful to recall the backdrop of reincarnation that lies behind all the Buddha's statements. The kind of patience he is referring to is not just a matter of keeping your temper when someone is late for an appointment; it is a deeply-rooted resolution not to swerve from dharma even in the face of a threat to life itself. Thus it connotes infinite compassion, unqualified good will for all creatures in all circumstances. In order to perfect such qualities, tradition tells us, the Bodhisattva or Buddha-to-be had to build up his endurance for many lives, strengthening his capacities with one-pointed determination.

This saga is said to have begun many thousands of incarnations ago in the Bodhisattva's life as Megha, a brahmin youth who met the great Dipankara, the Buddha of that age. So taken was he with this resplendent figure that Megha vowed he would undertake whatever disciplines might be required to become a Buddha himself, however many lives it might take. Interestingly enough, he also meets in that life a girl who exacts from him a vow that he will take her as his wife in every life – the future Yashodara. There is not space here to treat such Jatakas, or tales of the Buddha's previous births, in the depth they deserve; one can simply remark how they show the Bodhisattva's zeal in perfecting qualities such as patience and selfless courage, preparing him for final, complete awakening in his life as Prince Siddhartha.

From another point of view, however, the Buddha's story begins much earlier. The Bodhisattva's lives prior to human birth are narrated in the Jataka stories, which illustrate movingly why the Buddha exclaims that human birth is a rare privilege (182), gained only after many lives of undoing, as far as possible on that level, the primal instincts and urges of the animal realm. The Deer Jataka, for example, tells of the Bodhisattva's life as king of the Banyan deer, who offers his own life to a human king in order to save a pregnant doe from death. Sacrifice for others carries him one step nearer his goal. Whether he lives or dies is immaterial to him, for there will be countless other lives to come; the only question asked is how fully one has used life's precious opportunities for spiritual growth. Just as a human being, over billions of years, evolves biologically from a unicellular organism, the Buddha-to-be evolves spiritually into the Buddha by making the hard, unnatural effort to put others' welfare and safety before his own, in life after life, placing himself for an even greater leap next time.

The Buddha does not suggest that ordinary people try to imitate such intense feats of renunciation. Like a brilliant comet blazing in the sky, he inspires us but does not leave a personal trail (179). Ours is to catch fire from his example, as one lights a torch from a sacrificial fire (392).

Verses 190–192 refer to the Three Refuges of the Buddhist: the Buddha, the dharma, and the sangha. Driven by fear, people commonly seek reassurance from the world outside them; but in this transient world there is no refuge that is safe (188–189). The Three Refuges require one to turn inward, depending increasingly on oneself alone, for that is the path to freedom from fear.

The three are closely interrelated. "Taking refuge in the Buddha" does not mean expecting deliverance from him as a personal savior; it means following his example through the practice of his teachings: that is, by "taking refuge in the dharma." This in turn is most effectively done in the company of the sangha: those of like mind who are attempting to follow the same difficult path.

According to the Buddhist concept of *Trikaya*, literally "three bodies," there are three forms in which the Buddha

– or, more precisely, the Buddha-principle – is manifested throughout the universe as a refuge for all creatures.

First is *nirmanakaya*, that human form the Buddha-principle took on to answer the needs of a suffering world. The Gospel of John says, "And the Word became flesh and dwelt among us, full of grace and truth." The same principle is described in the Bhagavad Gita (4:7–8), where Lord Krishna says, "Whenever dharma declines and the purpose of life is forgotten, I manifest myself. I am born in age after age to protect the good, to destroy evil, and to reestablish dharma."

That particular Buddha born as Prince Siddhartha in Kapilavastu came to reinvigorate the religious practices of his time, which had calcified, on the one hand, into superstition and worship prompted by fear, and on the other hand into endless metaphysical speculation. This incarnation as the Buddha inspired an intense awakening in many peoples' hearts of spiritual self-reliance: the faith to look within oneself and take spiritual growth into one's own hands, independent of any outside influence.

When the Buddha shed his body, Buddhists would say, the nirmanakaya was reabsorbed into cosmic formlessness, and that particular chapter of his work which was dependent on his physical intervention came to an end. According to this doctrine, however, the Buddha was never merely an individual human being but, like St. John's Word or Logos, an eternal principle temporarily made flesh. Therefore, he cannot be said to have ceased to exist when his physical body died. He remains active in the world as a living force which continues to exercise a beneficial influence.

For his devotees, for example, the Buddha is still with us in his second form: the *sambhogakaya*, literally the "body of intense joy," a glorified manifestation of the Buddha's immense spiritual power and splendor which, like St. Teresa's visions of her Jesus, can be experientially revealed to those who earnestly practice his teachings. It is this "body of bliss" that the faithful pray to and attempt to represent in painting and sculpture. "Bliss" refers to the experience, testified to by the Buddha's followers, that when dharma is fully realized and assimilated into daily action, the mind is flooded with joy. The mystics of Mahayana Buddhism would add that if one is established in dharma at every level of awareness, from the everyday to the unconscious, then at the time of death this joy is not broken. This state is impossible to describe, but its promise is implicit in the Buddha's teachings, where it is placed within reach of all human beings.

Third and most abstract of the Buddha's forms is the *dharmakaya*, the "body of dharma." This is the cosmic aspect of the Buddha-principle, one with the Absolute, the unconditioned ground of every living creature. The Buddha may have shed his physical body, but the dharmakaya, the force he drew upon to set the wheel of dharma in motion, continues to operate. Never born, it can never die. Mahatma Gandhi said once that we can talk about a supreme reality either as the Lawgiver (*dharmakarta*) or as the Law (*dharma*). Similarly, the Buddha can be looked upon as embodied in the dharma that he taught: the law that all of life is one and indivisible.

The dharmakaya, however, is not an abstraction; it is the all-pervasive Buddha-principle acting throughout creation to relieve human distress. When the Buddha says in verse 5, for example, that "Hatred never ceases through hatred, only through love," he is, as he says, stating an "eternal law" which describes a binding, healing force. In the language of Buddhism, the Buddha is still active in the world in his "dharma body," inspiring and working through human instruments.

—S.R.

14 □: *The Awakened One*

179 He is the conqueror who can never be conquered,
into whose conquest no other can ever enter.
By what track can you reach him, the Buddha,
the awakened one, free of all conditioning?

180 How can you describe him in human language –
the Buddha, the awakened one, free from the net
of desires and the pollution of passions, free from
all conditioning?

181 Even the gods emulate those who are awakened.
Established in meditation, they live in freedom, at
peace.

182 It is hard to obtain human birth, harder to live
like a human being, harder still to understand the
dharma, but hardest of all to attain nirvana.

183 Avoid all evil, cultivate the good, purify your mind: this sums up the teaching of the Buddhas.

184 Cultivate the patience that endures, and attain nirvana, the highest goal of life. Do not oppress others or cause them pain; that is not the way of the spiritual aspirant.

185 Do not find fault with others, do not injure others, but live in accordance with the dharma. Be moderate in eating and sleeping, and meditate on the highest. This sums up the teaching of the Buddhas.

186 Even a shower of gold cannot quench the passions. They are wise who know that passions are passing and bring pain in their wake.

187 Even celestial pleasures cannot quench the passions. They are true followers of the Buddha who rejoice in the conquest of desires.

188 Driven by fear, people run for security to mountains and forests, to sacred spots and shrines. 189 But none of these can be a safe refuge, because they cannot free the mind from fear.

[190] Take refuge in the Buddha, the dharma, and the
sangha and you will grasp the Four Noble Truths:
[191] suffering, the cause of suffering, the end of
suffering, and the Noble Eightfold Path that takes
you beyond suffering. [192] That is your best refuge, your
only refuge. When you reach it, all sorrow falls away.

[193] One like the Buddha is hard to find; such a one
is not born everywhere. Where those established
in wisdom are born, the community flourishes.

[194] Blessed is the birth of the Buddha, blessed is the
teaching of the dharma; blessed is the sangha, where
all live in harmony.

[195-196] Blessed beyond measure are they who pay
homage to those worthy of homage: to the Buddha
and his disciples, who have gone beyond evil, shed all
fear, and crossed the river of sorrow to the other shore.

◘ *Joy*

THE PALI WORD *sukkha* (Sanskrit *su-kha*) is usually translated as happiness. As the opposite of *duhkha*, however, it connotes the end of all suffering, a state of being that is not subject to the ups and downs of change – that is, abiding joy.

It would be difficult to find a more thoroughly researched definition of joy than the Buddha's. If we can trust that at least the outline of truth remains in the legends of his life, then his questionings just before going forth to the Four Noble Sights were chiefly concerned with the search for absolute joy. What anyone could want of worldly happiness, Prince Siddhartha surely had, with the promise of much more. But the young prince scrutinized the content of worldly happiness much more closely than the rest of us, and his conclusion was that what people called joy was a house of cards perched precariously on certain preconditions. When these preconditions are fulfilled, the pleasure we feel lasts but a moment, for the nature of human experience is to change. And when they are not fulfilled, there is longing and a frustratingly elusive sense of loss; we grasp for what we do not have and nurse the gnawing desire to have it again. To try to hold on to anything – a thing, a person, an event, a position – merely exposes us to its loss. Anything that changes, the Buddha concluded, anything in our experience that consists of or is conditioned by component sensations – the Buddha's word was *samskaras* – produces sorrow, not joy. Experience promises happiness, but it delivers only constant change.

After the Four Noble Sights, Prince Siddhartha could not even enjoy natural beauty because he felt so keenly how swiftly it passes. Nor could he feel secure that the joy he took in his family would be lasting, once he had seen in his heart that change, disease, age, and death must come to all. He knew first-hand that a man can have everything and still be dissatisfied; but he had also seen – it was his fourth Noble Sight – that one can also have nothing and live in joy. Clearly joy was an internal state, with no necessary connection with external conditions.

Popular etymology sometimes derives *duhkha* from *duh*, a prefix meaning something wrong or evil, and *kha*, empty space. Ordinary experience is a void that cannot be filled by anything; it is nothing but change. Yet the Buddha, with his characteristic twist, proclaims that real joy can be found within that very stream of change. If one truly understands that life's very nature is change, then the burning desire to

wrest permanence from a world of passing sensations begins
to die; and as it dies, the mind begins to taste its natural state,
which is joy: not a sensation, but a state of consciousness
unaffected by pleasure and pain (373).

This is decidedly not a negative realization. Once we know
for certain what cannot give joy, we are ready for nirvana, the
highest joy (203). The path to joy lies not in depending on
external conditions, but in undoing the conditioning of pleasure and pain which excites the mind to search for satisfaction in the world outside. When the mind is stilled through
meditation, one drinks the joy of dharma, which lies beyond
the scope of anything conditioned (205).

It is worth mentioning that the Buddha classed all conditioned experience as duhkha, even the bliss of heavenly
realms sought by the orthodox devout. Just as in dreams one
can enjoy the sensations of worldly experience without the
fetters of space, time, and physical existence, the Buddha's
audience believed that in heavens like the "realm of the gods,"
those with favorable karma could satisfy desires uninhibited
by the harsh laws of worldly experience. But with or without a
body, experience is still conditioned; it cannot last. Even from
heaven one must be reborn in the world again, to learn to go
beyond the pleasure principle and attain life's goal, nirvana.
On the night before his illumination, the Buddha himself was
tempted by the subtle, intense joys of the deva-world when a
group of devas, prompted by Mara, offered to free him from

CHAPTER FIFTEEN

gross food and nourish him through the pores of his skin with heavenly nectars. Even these joys he spurned as obstacles in his path to nirvana. For him, joy is attainable on this very earth when a person purges himself of all impediments (200). The goal of life, attainable only on earth and in a body, gives the only joy the Buddha taught as lasting and worthy of all the effort required to attain it (381).

In this chapter the Buddha tells us how we can recognize those who have attained this inner joy: they live not to experience pleasure but to give, to relieve others' sorrows and return good for evil (197–198). One has only to think of the work of Mother Teresa of Calcutta to realize what the Buddha means in verse 198, or of Martin Luther King for verse 197. The Buddha was a stickler for verifying any spiritual attainment in adverse conditions, as well as for sharing its richness with those in the greatest need. When we find fulfillment in kindness, compassion, and selfless service, even when it means suffering, sorrow cannot touch us at all. And in the Buddha's terminology, when sorrow is absent, what remains is our native state: intense, abiding joy.

—S.R.

15 ⫶ *Joy*

197 Let us live in joy, never hating those who hate us.
Let us live in freedom, without hatred even among
those who hate.

198 Let us live in joy, never falling sick like those
who are sick. Let us live in freedom, without
disease even among those who are ill.

199 Let us live in joy, never attached among those
who are selfishly attached. Let us live in freedom
even among those who are bound by selfish
attachments.

200 Let us live in joy, never hoarding things among
those who hoard. Let us live in growing joy like the
bright gods.

²⁰¹ Conquest breeds hatred, for the conquered
live in sorrow. Let us be neither conqueror
nor conquered, and live in peace and joy.

²⁰² There is no fire like lust, no sickness like
hatred, no sorrow like separateness, no joy
like peace. ²⁰³No disease is worse than greed,
no suffering worse than selfish passion. Know
this, and seek nirvana as the highest joy.

²⁰⁴ Health is the best gift, contentment the best
wealth, trust the best kinsman, nirvana the greatest
joy. ²⁰⁵Drink the nectar of the dharma in the depths
of meditation, and become free from fear and sin.

²⁰⁶ It is good to meet the wise, even better to live
with them. But avoid the company of the immature
if you want joy.

²⁰⁷ Keeping company with the immature is like
going on a long journey with an enemy. The company
of the wise is joyful, like reunion with one's family.
²⁰⁸ Therefore, live among the wise, who are understanding, patient, responsible, and noble. Keep their
company as the moon moves among the stars.

CHAPTER SIXTEEN

◻: *Pleasure*

THE BUDDHA IS sometimes misinter-
preted as trying to squelch human affection in pursuit of
some impersonal spiritual ideal. Nothing could be further
from the truth. What he warns against in this chapter is not
affection as such, but self-centered attachment to what is personally pleasant.

Attachment to pleasure is one of the most serious obstacles
to spiritual growth. Aspirants can lose themselves in pleasure
and abandon their quest for life's supreme purpose (209); and
even if they continue to strive, they can get addicted to having
pleasant things and people around them, so that they cannot
face life's inevitable unpleasantnesses without suffering (210).
The person who sees life as it is understands that the pleasant
contains the unpleasant. Pleasant and unpleasant are not separate or separable; they are two sides of one experiential fact:
that life is change. This apparent paradox is well expressed in
Keats's "Ode on Melancholy":

> She dwells with Beauty – Beauty that must die;

And joy, whose hand is ever at his lips
Bidding adieu; and aching Pleasure nigh,
Turning to Poison while the bee-mouth sips:
Ay, in the very temple of delight
Veiled Melancholy has her sovran shrine . . .

What blocks spiritual growth is not pleasurable things and experiences themselves, but selfish attachment to them (211). In a Zen story, two monks approaching a river see a young woman who has no means of getting across. One of the monks carries her over and gently puts her down on the other side. On the way to the monastery, the other monk is so obsessed by what his friend has done that he can talk of nothing else. "A monk is not even supposed to touch a woman," he keeps saying, "let alone carry her around in his arms. What have you done?" Finally his friend puts an end to it. "I left that woman on the bank," he retorts. "You are still carrying her." In Buddhism, it is the mental state created by experience that is all-important. Without the emotional charge, the experience itself is insignificant. The Buddha would agree with the modern neuroscientist: we never really experience the world; we experience only our own nervous system.

All the dualities of human experience – pleasure and displeasure, praise and blame, success and defeat – produce suffering if we cannot face them with equanimity: that is, without the emotional response of attachment or aversion, which conditions us to crave or avoid such experiences the next time. In "Believing in Mind," Seng-ts'an, the Third Patriarch of Zen, conveys the loss one suffers by getting caught up in life's dualities:

> The Great Way knows no impediments;
> It does not pick and choose.
> When you abandon attachment and aversion
> You see it plainly;
> Make a thousandth of an inch distinction,
> Heaven and earth spring apart.
> If you want it to appear before your eyes,
> Cherish neither "for" nor "against."
> To compare what you like with what you dislike,
> That is the disease of the mind.
> Then you pass over the hidden meaning;
> Peace of mind is needlessly troubled.

The "hidden meaning," of things as they really are, lies beyond dualistic experience, waiting to be discovered by those who can travel upstream against conditioning (218).

The last two verses of this chapter, which bring in the concept of reincarnation, were the kind that the Buddha might have spoken to some village skeptic – someone wanting a guarantee that if he took to the Noble Eightfold Path and failed to attain nirvana, his effort would not go to waste. The Buddha likens his good deeds and spiritual practices to close relatives; just as his near ones wait to welcome him back from a long journey, his good deeds wait, and after death's long journey, they reward him with a splendid context for his next life (219–220). If he does not get far on the path in this life, the quest is simply suspended until he takes it up again in a new context: with conditions more suitable than his present ones, but otherwise exactly where he left off.

−S.R.

16 □ *Pleasure*

209 Don't run after pleasure and neglect the practice of meditation. If you forget the goal of life and get caught in the pleasures of the world, you will come to envy those who put meditation first.

210 Not seeing what is pleasant brings pain; seeing what is unpleasant brings pain. Therefore go beyond both pleasure and pain.

211 Don't get selfishly attached to anything, for trying to hold on to it will bring you pain. When you have neither likes nor dislikes, you will be free.

212 Selfish attachment brings suffering; selfish attachment brings fear. Be detached, and you will be free from suffering and fear.

213 Selfish bonds cause grief; selfish bonds cause fear.

Be unselfish, and you will be free from grief and fear.

²¹⁴ Selfish enjoyments lead to frustration; selfish enjoyments lead to fear. Be unselfish, and you will be free from frustration and fear.

²¹⁵ Selfish desires give rise to anxiety; selfish desires give rise to fear. Be unselfish, and you will be free from anxiety and fear.

²¹⁶ Craving brings pain; craving brings fear. Don't yield to cravings, and you will be free from pain and fear.

²¹⁷ Those who have character and discrimination, who are honest and good and follow the dharma with devotion, win the respect of all the world.

²¹⁸ If you long to know what is hard to know and can resist the temptations of the world, you will cross the river of life.

²¹⁹⁻²²⁰ As your family and friends receive you with joy when you return from a long journey, so will your good deeds receive you when you go from this life to the next, where they will be waiting for you with joy like your kinsmen.

CHAPTER SEVENTEEN

▣ *Anger*

THE BUDDHA IS not among those who praise "righteous indignation." When he exhorts us to give up anger, he does not list under what specific conditions this should be done: it should simply be given up, and that is all. His concern is with mental states, and since an angry mind is out of control, the Buddha naturally counsels against it. Even if getting angry gives a sense of triumph or seems to ease pent-up tensions, anger is linked with duhkha, suffering. Free yourself from anger, the Buddha says, and duhkha cannot touch you (221). Since freedom from duhkha is the goal of his entire teaching, he puts a high priority on the conquest of anger.

Mahatma Gandhi offers his own example of how the energy dissipated in anger can be conserved and harnessed for a selfless goal:

> I have learnt through bitter experience the one supreme lesson to conserve my anger, and as heat conserved is

transmuted into energy, even so our anger controlled can
be transmuted into a power which can move the world.

Anger is controlled by "non-anger," here translated as gentleness or compassion (223). If a person is on the point of an angry outburst, the Buddha expects him to try to brake it, just as a driver would brake a fast-moving chariot (222). But a more practical solution is not to let anger arise. As a supreme physician, the Buddha takes a preventive approach. In the same way that anger becomes part of personality by indulging one's temper over and over and over, anger can be removed from personality by cultivating gentleness, compassion, and patience, all of which are part of what "non-anger" means. The complete absence of anger, resentment, and hostility, then, is not a negative state of repression; it is a very positive state, as Gandhi implies, and full of power.

Non-anger begins with right conduct, the control of one's body and actions – for example, not striking another person out of anger. Simultaneously, though generally with greater difficulty, one strives for right speech, never uttering harsh words (232). But most difficult is eliminating anger from the mind. When one has finally ceased even to think angry thoughts, even in sleep, anger has been erased completely. What remains is the Unconditioned: consciousness in its natural state.

In the context of a comprehensive spiritual program with a supreme goal, this kind of discipline is not repression.

Psychologists rightly caution that repression of anger can have disastrous physical and emotional consequences. On the Eightfold Path, however, we are not asked to repress anger but to learn to channel its raw power before it explodes in an outburst of destructive behavior, drawing on that power for spiritual growth.

Always a pragmatist, the Buddha even goes to the extent of saying that he would welcome an outburst of anger if it really could help bring an end to suffering. It is precisely because it does not help end suffering that he urges us to curb anger at its source. The Zen poet Han-shan of Tang dynasty China said:

> Anger is fire in the mind
> Burning up the forest of your merits and blessings.
> If you want to walk in the path of the bodhisattvas,
> Endure insults and guard your mind against anger.

Mastery of the practice of non-anger thus ends in the precious capacity to return love for abuse, an ideal of all the world's major religions.

—S.R.

17 ▯ *Anger*

²²¹ Give up anger, give up pride, and free yourself
from worldly bondage. No sorrow can befall
those who never try to possess people and things
as their own.

²²² Those who hold back rising anger like a rolling
chariot are real charioteers. Others merely hold the
reins.

²²³ Conquer anger through gentleness, unkindness
through kindness, greed through generosity, and
falsehood by truth. ²²⁴Be truthful; do not yield to
anger. Give freely, even if you have but little. The gods
will bless you.

²²⁵ Injuring no one, self-controlled, the wise enter the
state of peace beyond all sorrow. ²²⁶ Those who are
vigilant, who train their minds day and night and

strive continually for nirvana, enter the state of peace beyond all selfish passions.

[227] There is an old saying: "People will blame you if you say too much; they will blame you if you say too little; they will blame you if you say just enough." No one in this world escapes blame.

[228] There never was and never will be anyone who receives all praise or all blame. [229-230] But who can blame those who are pure, wise, good, and meditative? They shine like a coin of pure gold. Even the gods praise them, even Brahma the Creator.

[231] Use your body for doing good, not for harm. Train it to follow the dharma. [232] Use your tongue for doing good, not for harm. Train it to speak kindly. [233] Use your mind for doing good, not for harm. Train your mind in love. [234] The wise are disciplined in body, speech, and mind. They are well controlled indeed.

CHAPTER EIGHTEEN

ⓘ *Impurity*

THE BRILLIANT THERAVADA com-
mentator Buddhaghosa, in a precise, detailed work called *The
Path of Purification* (XXII.61), specifies three basic kinds of
impurity: greed, hatred, and infatuation. "They are known
as impurities," he explains, "because they are dirty themselves, like oil and mud, and because they dirty other things."
Because personality is a process, an impurity spreads, cor-
rupting other traits little by little.

The Buddha's examples elucidate this idea further. The
body loses health when it does not get enough exercise; therefore indolence is an impurity in physical health. A house dete-
riorates when one does not take care of it; carelessness ruins
the work of a watchman; stingy reservations taint even a lav-
ish gift (241–242). An impurity, in other words, is any habit,
mistake, or foible that corrodes or coarsens something good.
Gradually, through the continual production of unfavorable
karma, it eats away at personality as a spot of rust corrodes a
piece of iron (240). The worst of all such taints is ignorance,

because it prevents us from seeing other impurities that consume us from within (243).

As always, the Buddha contrasts the consequences of two opposite choices. If we do nothing to remove impurities from our character, the habits they foster will grow stronger. Eventually they cannot help outstripping our will, so that we have no protection against serious lapses of judgment which will gradually drain us of vitality and health (246–248). Rather than face death in such a condition, the Buddha exhorts us, it is better to strive to remove impurities little by little every day, as a smith gradually removes the dross from silver (239). Once free from all impurities, we are an island unto ourselves, beyond the reach of corrosion.

The key concept here is *ashrava,* translated as "compulsion" in verse 253. Its literal meaning, "outflow," suggests a compulsive, only partially conscious seepage of vitality and mental energy into external desires and activities. Like toothpaste squeezed inadvertently from a tube, energy drained by an ashrava has nowhere to go but out; it is completely wasted. The example given here is focusing compulsively on another's faults and becoming angered by them – an activity which consumes a good deal of energy but accomplishes nothing. Other examples might be any compulsive habit or strong, obsessive desire.

But *ashrava* has another connotation, for the word also refers to an intoxicating beverage extracted from flowers or trees. On his tours through village India, the Buddha must have become familiar with the way in which coconut milk is hung out in pots from the trees to ferment, producing a toddy that many villagers still drink after a hard day in the fields. Always alive to the range of experience in his audience, the Buddha may have had this connotation in mind when he chose the word *ashrava* to describe the genesis of an impure mental state, which goes on fermenting in consciousness and transforming more and more of the mind. Resentment and fixation on others' faults is a perfect example of how a heady ashrava can brew in the unconscious until a person reels under its influence, losing control whenever a situation or person provokes him. Practice of right speech and right conduct are essential steps in stopping this fermenting process.

—S.R.

18 ◻ *Impurity*

²³⁵ You are like a withered leaf, waiting for the
messenger of death. You are about to go on a long
journey, but you are so unprepared. ²³⁶ Light the
lamp within; strive hard to attain wisdom. Become
pure and innocent, and live in the world of light.

²³⁷ Your life has come to an end, and you are in the
presence of death. There is no place to rest on this
journey, and you are so unprepared. ²³⁸ Light the lamp
within; strive hard to attain wisdom. Become pure and
innocent, and you will be free from birth and death.

²³⁹ Make your mind pure as a silversmith blows
away the impurities of silver, little by little, instant
by instant. ²⁴⁰ As rust consumes the iron which
breeds it, evil deeds consume those who do them.

²⁴¹ The mantram is weak when not repeated;
a house falls into ruin when not repaired; the
body loses health when it is not exercised;
the watchman fails when vigilance is lost.

²⁴² Lack of modesty is a drawback in women; lack
of generosity taints those who give. ²⁴³ Selfish deeds
are without merit here and hereafter. But there
is no impurity greater than ignorance. Remove
that through wisdom and you will be pure.

²⁴⁴ Life seems easy for one without shame, no better
than a crow, a mischief-maker who is insolent and
dissolute. ²⁴⁵ Life is hard for one who is humble,
gentle, and detached, who tries to live in purity.

²⁴⁶ They dig their own graves who kill, lie, get drunk,
or covet the wealth or spouse of another. ²⁴⁷ Those who
drink to intoxication are digging up their own roots.
²⁴⁸ Any indiscipline brings evil in its wake. Know this,
and do not let greed and vice bring you lingering pain.

²⁴⁹ Some give out of faith, others out of friendship.
Do not envy others for the gifts they receive, or
you will have no peace of mind by day or night.

²⁵⁰ Those who have destroyed the roots of jealousy
have peace of mind always.

²⁵¹ There is no fire like lust, no jailer like hate,
no snare like infatuation, no torrent like greed.

²⁵² It is easy to see the faults of others; we winnow
them like chaff. It is hard to see our own; we
hide them as a gambler hides a losing draw.

²⁵³ But when one keeps dwelling on the faults
of others, his own compulsions grow worse,
making it harder to overcome them.

²⁵⁴ There is no path in the sky; there is no
refuge in the world for those driven by their
desires. But the disciples of the Buddha live in
freedom. ²⁵⁵ There is no path in the sky; there
is no refuge in the world for those driven by
their desires. All is change in the world, but the
disciples of the Buddha are never shaken.

▯: *Established in Dharma*

THE SUBJECT OF this chapter is the person whose life has become established in dharma. But the word here has a fuller connotation than the Buddha's Eightfold Path, for dharma was an ancient concept in India even when the Buddha was born. The word probably comes from the root *dhri,* "to support." Volumes have been written on the different meanings it has acquired, but from a practical standpoint the core meaning is simply "that which supports." Dharma is the very underpinning of existence, the underlying unity of life, the essential support of all; it stands for the cosmic order – the order of an indivisible whole – and therefore for the moral order in human life, and so it also means "law" in the sense of a central law of creation. When the Buddha saw the workings of dharma in his cosmic ecstasy under the bodhi tree, he chose this word to describe the goal of human life: not Self-realization or union with God, but simply living in complete harmony with life's cosmic interdependence. In this chapter he describes the person who lives a life nourished by the dharma, as well as the one who flouts it.

Many verses reiterate that living in harmony with dharma has nothing to do with external appearances or social position. A person who speaks on the dharma with eloquence and conviction is not necessarily established in it (258–259); even a monk or *bhikshu* should not be considered established in dharma by virtue of vows alone (264, 266). Similarly, a *thera* or elder does not earn this title just by the graying of his hair (260). The true follower of the dharma is that person who has passed beyond the reach of good and evil (267): that is, who no longer has to deliberate between right and wrong; harmony with the dharma is as natural and necessary as breathing. And if one is truly an elder, conduct will surely show it, for such a person will be free from all impurity (261). The Buddha despised any religious authority due solely to position, particularly if the person was corrupt. For him, authority emanated only from true spiritual attainment.

The Buddha's qualifications for an upholder of dharma are given in verse 259. One need not preach the dharma eloquently nor even hear it preached often. What is important is that meditation be deep enough to see dharma's cosmic order and align one's conduct with it. This is a very rare attainment, for it means that self-will – the insistent urge to pursue one's own desires instead of living for the whole – has to be extinguished. For the Buddha, however, nothing could substitute

for the direct experience of meditation. "Do not accept something merely from tradition or out of blind faith," he says. "Do
not accept it even on the word of your teacher. *Ehi passika*:
go and see for yourself, through the practice of meditation."
To be established in dharma means not only seeing it face to
face in enlightenment, but repeating the experience over and
over until unity is more real than the passing show we know
through the senses. Only then will one's actions never fall
back into the tyranny of lower laws (364).

A person who understands the reason behind a law is
more likely to obey it intelligently than someone who is simply ordered to obey. Similarly, the person who sees life inter-
dependently linked in dharma's cosmic web will know exactly
why controlling selfish urges is essential in conduct; there will
be no need to take someone else's word for it. It is through
direct, intimate, personal knowledge of dharma, rather than
a high moral code or social pressure, that selfless, righteous
actions arise.

—S.R.

19 ◻: *Established in Dharma*

256–257 They are not following dharma who resort to
violence to achieve their purpose. But those who lead
others through nonviolent means, knowing right
and wrong, may be called guardians of the dharma.

258 One is not wise because he talks a good deal. They
are wise who are patient, and free from hate and fear.

259 Dharma is not upheld by talking about
it. Dharma is upheld by living in harmony
with it, even if one is not learned.

260 Gray hair does not make an elder; one can grow
old and still be immature. **261** A true elder is truthful,
virtuous, gentle, self-controlled, and pure in mind.

²⁶² Neither pleasant words nor a pretty face can make beautiful a person who is jealous, selfish, or deceitful. ²⁶³ Only those who have uprooted such impurities from the mind are fit to be called beautiful.

²⁶⁴ Shaving one's head cannot make a monk of one who is undisciplined, untruthful, and driven by selfish desires. ²⁶⁵ He is a real monk who has extinguished all selfish desires, large and small.

²⁶⁶ Begging alms does not make a bhikshu; one must follow the dharma completely. ²⁶⁷ He is a true bhikshu who is chaste and beyond the reach of good and evil, who passes through the world with detachment.

²⁶⁸⁻²⁶⁹ Observing silence cannot make a sage of one who is ignorant and immature. He is wise who, holding the scales, chooses the good and avoids the bad.

²⁷⁰ One is not noble who injures living creatures. They are noble who hurt no one.

271-272 Not by rituals and resolutions, nor by much
learning, nor by celibacy, nor even by meditation
can you find the supreme, immortal joy of nirvana
until you have extinguished your self-will.

CHAPTER TWENTY

❏: *The Path*

THE BUDDHIST PALI canon is several
times as long as the Old and New Testaments combined, yet
not even a fraction of this literature directly deals with the
steps of the Buddha's Eightfold Path. Instead there is much
discussion of insights attained on that path, and the philosophical doctrines derived from those insights – so much, in
fact, that the reader of Buddhist scriptures might tend to forget that the actual practice of the Eightfold Path was the Buddha's central teaching. It is, he assures us, the same path that
he himself traveled to reach the end of suffering (275). Had it
not been practiced and mastered, by him and many others,
there would have been no one to make the dazzling insights
of later Buddhist philosophy.

One of the reasons so little is said about the Eightfold Path
is the highly intellectual bent of many Buddhist thinkers,
who might have found matters like right occupation rather
mundane. Another explanation may be the fact that until
very recent times, practical spiritual instruction in India has

always been oral, direct from teacher to student, so that in any case we should not expect to find written instruction in the Eightfold Path. Whatever the explanation, the Path remains far more important than the philosophy. It is, in the Buddha's own estimation, his foremost gift to mankind.

That being said, one must also note that three of the most philosophically significant verses in the Dhammapada occur in this chapter. Verses 277 through 279 present the three marks or characteristics of all conditioned things (*samskaras*): impermanence (*anitya*), suffering (*duhkha*), and the absence of a personal self (*anatman*). Right understanding, the first step on the Eightfold Path, means seeing clearly that such flaws are an inescapable part of every human experience. The other seven steps are there to enable us to build our lives on the only foundation that endures, the dharma.

–S.R.

20 ॥ *The Path*

²⁷³ Of paths the Eightfold is the best; of truths the
Noble Four are best; of mental states, detachment is
the best; of human beings the illumined one is best.

²⁷⁴ This is the path; there is no other that leads to
the purification of the mind. Follow this path and
conquer Mara. This is the path; there is no other that
leads to the purification of the mind. ²⁷⁵ This path
will lead to the end of suffering. This is the path I
made known after the arrows of sorrow fell away.

²⁷⁶ All the effort must be made by you; Buddhas
only show the way. Follow this path and practice
meditation; go beyond the power of Mara.

²⁷⁷ All created things are transitory; those
who realize this are freed from suffering. This
is the path that leads to pure wisdom.

278 All created beings are involved in sorrow;
those who realize this are freed from suffering.
This is the path that leads to pure wisdom.

279 All states are without self; those who
realize this are freed from suffering. This
is the path that leads to pure wisdom.

280 Now is the time to wake up, when you
are young and strong. Those who wait and
aver, with a weak will and a divided mind,
will never find the way to pure wisdom.

281 Guard your thoughts, words, and
deeds. These three disciplines will speed
you along the path to pure wisdom.

282 Meditation brings wisdom; lack of meditation
leaves ignorance. Know well what leads
you forward and what holds you back, and
choose the path that leads to wisdom.

283 Cut down the whole forest of selfish desires,
not just one tree only. Cut down the whole forest
and you will be on your way to liberation.

²⁸⁴ If there is any trace of lust in your mind, you
are bound to life like a suckling calf to its mother.
²⁸⁵ Pull out every selfish desire as you would an
autumn lotus with your hand. Follow the path
to nirvana with a guide who knows the way.

²⁸⁶ "I will make this my winter home, have
another house for the monsoon, and dwell
in a third during the summer." Lost in such
fancies, one forgets his final destination.

²⁸⁷ Death comes and carries off a man absorbed
in his family and possessions as the monsoon
flood sweeps away a sleeping village.

²⁸⁸ Neither children nor parents can rescue one
whom death has seized. ²⁸⁹ Remember this, and
follow without delay the path that leads to nirvana.

CHAPTER TWENTY-ONE

❏: *Varied Verses*

THE OPENING VERSE of this chapter gives the entire theme of the Dhammapada. Its message is not confined to ancient India, nor does it end with the Buddha's times, because it embodies his pragmatic spirit:

> If one who enjoys a lesser happiness beholds a greater one,
> let him leave aside the lesser to gain the greater.

Growing up in luxury, with the opportunity to taste all life's pleasures, the Buddha does not deny that they can bring a measure of transient happiness. But faced with the choice between such a small happiness and the vastly greater happiness of an intentional life and a well-trained mind, he says, any intelligent human being would forsake the lesser to enjoy the greater. The rest of the Dhammapada only elaborates this choice and helps us choose with wisdom and full resolve.

The last six verses of this otherwise miscellaneous chapter are some of the most lyrical in the Dhammapada. They give a memorable picture of the "greater happiness" of those who follow the Noble Eightfold Path:

> The disciples of Gautama are wide awake and vigilant,
> absorbed in the dharma day and night.
>
> . . .
>
> The disciples of Gautama are wide awake and vigilant,
> rejoicing in compassion day and night.
>
> . . .
>
> The disciples of Gautama are wide awake and vigilant,
> rejoicing in meditation day and night. (297, 300–301)

To the Western reader, nothing could be more reminiscent of the joyful brotherhood of the early disciples of St. Francis.

–S.R.

21 ॥ *Varied Verses*

²⁹⁰ If one who enjoys a lesser happiness beholds a
greater one, let him leave aside the lesser to gain
the greater.

²⁹¹ Don't try to build your happiness on the
unhappiness of others. You will be enmeshed in
a net of hatred.

²⁹² Do not fail to do what ought to be done, and do not
do what ought not to be done. Otherwise your burden
of suffering will grow heavier. ²⁹³ Those who meditate
and keep their senses under control never fail to do
what ought to be done, and never do what ought not
to be done. Their suffering will come to an end.

²⁹⁴ Kill mother lust and father self-will, kill the
kings of carnal passions, and you will be freed
from sin. ²⁹⁵ The true brahmin has killed mother

lust and father self-will; he has killed the kings
of carnal passions and the ego that obstructs
him on the path. Such a one is freed from sin.

296 The disciples of Gautama are wide awake and
vigilant, with their thoughts focused on the Buddha
day and night.

297 The disciples of Gautama are wide awake and
vigilant, absorbed in the dharma day and night.

298 The disciples of Gautama are wide awake and
vigilant, with their thoughts focused on the sangha
day and night.

299 The disciples of Gautama are wide awake and
vigilant, with their thoughts focused on sense-
training day and night.

300 The disciples of Gautama are wide awake and
vigilant, rejoicing in compassion day and night.

301 The disciples of Gautama are wide awake and
vigilant, rejoicing in meditation day and night.

³⁰² It is hard to leave the world and hard to
live in it, painful to live with the worldly and
painful to be a wanderer. Reach the goal;
you will wander and suffer no more.

³⁰³ Those who are good and pure in conduct are
honored wherever they go. ³⁰⁴ The good shine like
the Himalayas, whose peaks glisten above the
rest of the world even when seen from a distance.
Others pass unseen, like an arrow shot at night.

³⁰⁵ Sitting alone, sleeping alone, going about alone,
vanquish the ego by yourself alone. Abiding joy
will be yours when all selfish desires end.

CHAPTER TWENTY-TWO

▫ *The Downward Course*

THE TORMENTS OF hell have exer-
cised a strong hold over orthodox believers in all religions.
Buddhism, which alludes to hell often, is no exception, and
the descriptions in some of the later scriptures are gruesome
enough to rival any of the horrors familiar in the Christian
tradition. The one difference is that in Buddhism the sinner
does not go to eternal damnation. Perhaps the only fortunate
thing about the Buddha's concept of impermanence is that it
extends to all states: hell, like heaven, is not lasting. A person
remains there, suffering intensely, only until the unfavorable
karma from past evil deeds is exhausted. Then that person is
reborn again on earth, with a fresh opportunity to learn that
actions which harm life contain the seeds of their own punishment. Hell in Buddhism really is educative, not vengeful,
and it is not the sentence of a wrathful deity but the natural,
unavoidable result of actions that violate dharma. Suffering
drives home the lesson that certain ways of living bring pain
to oneself as well as to others, because life is an indivisible

whole; after that lesson, one gets the opportunity to correct one's direction in a new life.

Hell, in other words, embodies and intensifies the truth of duhkha. For someone who understands that a life prompted by selfish conditioning has to involve duhkha, suffering is inherent in any experience conditioned by karma. Such a person is more sensitive to the nature of life than the majority who believe that pleasure can be pursued without pain, and that very sensitivity means greater responsibility and greater anguish if one slips. For someone committed to the spiritual life, the pain of having committed a serious mistake can be so excruciating that it is hell here on earth; no reference to another world is necessary. As in the case of someone who commits adultery (309–310), suffering need not occur in the punishment of some afterlife; it creates its own hell in the minds of those involved.

The real significance of hell is that it is a mental state caused by the content of a person's own thoughts and actions. Wrong actions bring their own punishment, whether from within or from without, or, most tragically, by damaging one's hard-won spiritual progress.

"The mind is its own place," Milton says in *Paradise Lost*, "and in itself / Can make a heaven of hell or hell of heaven." In an ancient Indian story, a king called Vipashchit breathed his last and journeyed to the afterlife. He had been such a kind ruler, a model for all kings, that the devas in heaven were all anxious to set him up as their teacher and guide. When he reached his destination, he was welcomed with smiles and embraces and even tears of gratitude.

Some time passed, and Vipashchit settled down in satisfaction to his new life. Heaven, he remarked to one of his new companions, was a happier place than even he had ever dreamed it could be. "Heaven?" the man replied. "This isn't heaven, your majesty! This is hell. The people here are miserable. But in your presence their suffering turns to joy."

Just then some heavenly messengers arrived with abject apologies; a terrible mistake had been made. "All of us in Heaven are waiting for you, O Great King," they said.

Vipashchit looked around and smiled. "I am staying here," he replied. "I have already found my heaven."

The mental state is paramount; it can make life hell or heaven whatever the surroundings. The kind of experience one undergoes depends on the choices one makes. As always, the Buddha leaves this up to each individual.

—S.R.

22 ❦ *The Downward Course*

306 One who says what is not true, one who denies
what he has done, both choose the downward course.
After death these two become partners in falsehood.

307 Those who put on the saffron robe but remain
ill-mannered and undisciplined are dragged
down by their evil deeds. 308 It is better for an
undisciplined monk to swallow a red-hot ball of
iron than to live on the charity of the devout.

309 Adultery leads to loss of merit, loss of sleep,
condemnation, and increasing suffering. 310 On
this downward course, what pleasure can there
be for the frightened lying in the arms of the
frightened, both going in fear of punishment?
Therefore do not commit adultery.

³¹¹ As a blade of kusha grass can cut the finger when
it is wrongly held, asceticism practiced without
discrimination can send one on the downward course.

³¹² An act performed carelessly, a vow not kept,
a code of chastity not strictly observed: these
things bring little reward. ³¹³ If anything is worth
doing, do it with all your heart. A half-hearted
ascetic covers himself with more and more dust.

³¹⁴ Refrain from evil deeds, which cause suffering later.
Perform good deeds, which can cause no suffering.
³¹⁵ Guard yourself well, both within and without,
like a well-defended fort. Don't waste a moment, for
wasted moments send you on the downward course.

Those who are ashamed of deeds they
should not be ashamed of, and not ashamed
of deeds they should be ashamed of, follow
false doctrines on the downward course.

³¹⁷ Those who fear what they ought not to fear,
and do not fear what they ought to fear, follow
false doctrines on the downward course.

[318] Those who see wrong where there is none,
and do not see wrong where there is, follow
false doctrines on the downward course.

[319] But those who see wrong where there is
wrong, and see no wrong where there is none,
follow true doctrines on the upward course.

◻: The Elephant

THROUGHOUT INDIAN scripture and folkfore, the elephant ranks first among all animals in importance. And no wonder: for many centuries, the Indian people had trained elephants to lift and transport burdens much heavier than the human being or any other draft animal could manage, as they still do today in the Indian timber industry. The trained elephant, highly intelligent and fiercely loyal, also played a decisive role on the battlefield, and from the time of the Buddha onwards they were considered the most important division of an Indian army.

In this chapter the Buddha plays off *danta*, "trained" or "self-restrained," with *danti*, one of the common names for the elephant. With its strength, endurance, gentleness, and remarkable restraint, the elephant has long symbolized to the Indian mind the enormous power locked up within every human being. Just as an elephant can uproot a tree, wrap its trunk around it, and carry it like a toy, the human being, the Buddha says, can gain access to immense resources of health,

energy, patience, and power through the disciplines of the
Eightfold Path. The Buddha himself was called "the Great Elephant." By taking the analogy of the trained elephant, whose
immense power has been transformed into loving human
service, he manages to convey to his Indian audience both the
difficulty and the rewards of spiritual discipline.

—S.R.

23 ¤: *The Elephant*

³²⁰ Patiently I shall bear harsh words as the
elephant bears arrows on the battlefield. People
are often inconsiderate.

³²¹ Only a trained elephant goes to the battlefield;
only a trained elephant carries the king. Best
among men are those who have trained the
mind to endure harsh words patiently.

³²² Mules are good animals when trained; even better
are well-trained Sind horses and great elephants.
Best among men is one with a well-trained mind.

³²³ No animal can take you to nirvana; only a well-
trained mind can lead you to this untrodden land.

324 The elephant Dhanapalaka in heat will not eat at all when he is bound; he pines for his mate in the elephant grove.

325 Eating too much, sleeping too much, like an overfed hog, those too lazy to exert effort are born again and again.

326 Long ago my mind used to wander as it liked and do what it wanted. Now I can rule my mind as the mahout controls the elephant with his hooked staff.

327 Be vigilant; guard your mind against negative thoughts. Pull yourself out of bad ways as an elephant raises itself out of the mud.

328 If you find a friend who is good, wise, and loving, walk with him all the way and overcome all dangers.

329 If you cannot find a friend who is good, wise, and loving, walk alone, like a king who has renounced his kingdom or an elephant roaming at will in the forest. 330 It is better to be alone than to live with the immature. Be contented, and walk alone like an elephant roaming in the forest. Turn away from evil.

[331] It is good to have friends when friendship is mutual. Good deeds are friends at the time of death. But best of all is going beyond sorrow.

[332] It is good to be a mother, good to be a father, good to be one who follows the dharma. But best of all is to be an illumined sage.

[333] It is good to live in virtue, good to have faith, good to attain the highest wisdom, good to be pure in heart and mind. Joy will be yours always.

◩: *Thirst*

IT HAS BEEN said that Buddhism is essentially a psychology of desire. The second Noble Truth proclaims selfish desire or craving as the cause of all the suffering in life, and its importance in Buddhist thought is evident in the fact that the Buddha uses at least fifteen terms for it. The chief of these is *trishna*, which literally means "thirst." It is an apt word, for in a tropical country like India, the intense craving for water on a scorching, dry day makes a vivid metaphor for the fiercest of human drives.

Trishna is that force which drives all creatures to seek personal satisfaction of their urges at any cost, even at the expense of others. It is the deadliest and subtlest of snares because its gratification almost always brings a surge of satisfaction, reinforcing the compulsion to act on that desire again. It is only later that the consequences of pursuing self-centered desires begin to burn like coals smoldering under the ashes (71).

Any action undertaken for personal aggrandizement, any human activity or institution that promotes one person or group at the expense of any other, the Buddha would trace to the root cause of selfish desire. As often, the determining factor is the mental state behind the activity – the motivation of profit, power, pleasure, prestige, possession – even more than the activity itself.

In Buddhist psychology, each desire is an isolated moment of mental activity – a *dharma*, in the Buddhist's technical vocabulary – rising up in the mind. It can be ignored, or one can choose to yield to it. If one yields, the next wave of desire will have greater power to compel attention, and the mental agitation it causes will be more intense. On the other hand, if one chooses to defy a strong desire, the pain can be considerable. "Know me to be the power called Thirst," Trishna demands of the Buddha on the eve of his enlightenment, "and give me my due of worship. Otherwise I will squeeze you with all my might and wring out the last of your life!" However, if one succeeds in not giving in to selfish desires as they arise, the mind gradually quiets down, leaving a longer and longer interval between waves of desire in which the mind is calm. This calmness is our natural birthright, a state beyond the suffering entangled with desire. All the Buddha's teachings come round to this one practical point: to find permanent joy, we have to learn how not to yield to selfish desire.

This conclusion is so contrary to human nature that it is not surprising to hear even experts maintain that in preaching the extinction of desire, the Buddha was denying everything that makes life worth living. But *trishna* does not mean all desire; it means *selfish* desire, the conditioned craving for self-aggrandizement. Far from denigrating desire, the Buddha knew it is the power of desire that fuels progress on the Noble Eightfold Path. He distinguishes raw, unregulated, self-directed trishna from the unselfish and uplifting desire to dissolve one's egotism in selfless service of all. The person who makes no effort to go against the base craving for personal satisfaction is headed for more bondage and more sorrow (349); but he can transform such cravings into *virya*, vigor, which is intense desire directed toward spiritual growth:

> If, while holding on to concentration and one-pointedness of mind, one emphasizes desire, that is concentration of desire. One generates desire for the non-arising of unwholesome states that have not yet arisen; he puts forth effort and mobilizes energy.... He generates desire for the arising of wholesome states that have not yet arisen; he puts forth effort and mobilizes energy. (*Samyutta Nikaya* v.268)
>
> Therefore, mobilize vigor to attain what is unattained, to master what is unmastered, to realize what is unrealized. In this way your taking to the spiritual life will not be barren, but fruitful and ever-growing. (*Samyutta Nikaya* 11.29)

How could such intense effort be made without desire? Spiritual dynamics is not a matter of crushing base desires but of transforming them, drawing on their power to master the Eightfold Path.

The Buddha divides trishna into three categories:

> It is selfish desire, bound up with passion and greed, which
> produces separate existence and leads to future births, and
> which keeps lingering pleasurably here and there: that is,
> the desire for sense pleasure (*kama-trishna*), the desire for
> birth in a world of separateness (*bhava-trishna*), and the
> desire for extinction (*vibhava-trishna*).
>
> (*Samyutta Nikaya* v.421)

The most obvious of these, of course, is the craving for
sense pleasure, which the Buddha explains as the force of
desire attaching itself to objects in the external world (341).
Any craving for an experience that one thinks will add to
personal pleasure, comfort, or happiness is an expression of
kama-trishna, whose soft bonds to objects of sensory satisfaction are stronger than iron chains or fetters of wood or rope
(345). Even of himself, the Buddha says that if he had had to
contend with another desire as strong as that of sex – the most
powerful expression of kama-trishna – then he would not
have been able to achieve his goal. Mara is the personification
of the strong hold such desires have (7).

The other two kinds of craving are opposing drives deep
in the human unconscious: bhava-trishna, toward existence
as a separate creature; vibhava-trishna, toward extinguish-
ing that existence. Bhava-trishna is the urge to go on uphold-
ing and strengthening one's individuality, in pursuit not only

of wealth, fame, and power but also of beliefs, opinions, and dogmas.

With virtually everyone driven by the craving for personal aggrandizement and sensory satisfaction, it is obvious that there will be clashes as egos collide. The Buddha would trace every conflict, even war, back to these basic selfish drives, occasionally couched in self-righteous language or elevated into national or corporate policies. This is another reason the Buddha maintained that peace is best served by individuals taking in earnest to his Eightfold Path. The more people there are who understand the central role that selfish desire plays in human motivation and behavior, the more intelligently its disastrous effects can be mitigated. A deeper and fuller knowledge of one's own inner dynamics of desire helps in developing right understanding of world conflicts.

The Buddha takes the thirst for personal aggrandizement even beyond the international sphere. Trishna has no self-limiting principle; the more it is fed, the higher it will flame. It cannot be terminated just by satisfying the desires of one lifetime. According to the Tibetan Book of the Dead, these desires remain in consciousness at death. Because of their power, they condition the choice of a new context for another life, where satisfaction of the same desires will again be pursued. As long as it remains in consciousness, the master desire for more worldly experience will go on generating more desires, even if some of them seem to be brought under control. Like a monkey swinging from tree to tree in the forest, the Buddha says, desires keep us leaping from life to life pursuing ever-elusive satisfaction (334). In other discourses he personifies the deep desire for separate satisfaction as an enterprising seamstress, sewing one life to another and still another with her endless supply of desires.

The third kind of selfish desire, vibhava-trishna, is the craving to end existence, the very opposite of the drive to go on experiencing and self-building. But this is far from the desire for nirvana, the release from the cycle of birth and death. Nirvana is release from trishna itself, from the torment and conditioning of selfish desire; its characteristic features are joy, vitality, good health, and the highest of all purposes in life, the desire and capacity to give – all the things that make life worth living. Vibhava-trishna, by contrast, is the oppressive desire for self-oblivion or self-destruction, prompted in Buddhist psychology by the revulsion with life that comes as the fruits of selfishness turn rotten or bitter. This self-destructive urge is often not consciously expressed, but when it does find expression, it in no way ends one's separate existence; it only draws a temporary cover of oblivion over the burdens and stresses of selfish behavior. A person who jumps off a bridge to end his life, the Buddha would say, simply gets reborn to face the same desperate situation all over again.

In Buddhist psychology, any activity that is potentially

self-destructive stems from the urge for extinction. Even that second double martini intended to deaden the strains of the day is an example of the urge to escape oneself for a few hours. This desire for extinction is present in everyone, but in a normal, healthy person it is held in balance by the desire for becoming.

Verse 353, one of the most famous in all Buddhism, shows that the Buddha was a humble man but not a modest one. He is well aware of the difficulty and significance of his stupendous accomplishments, which he has achieved with no help apart from his own efforts. Because he had no teacher, some have claimed that he tried to lessen the bond to the guru so prized in Hinduism. Certainly he put the greatest of faith in self-effort, but that is essential on the spiritual path in any religion, with a teacher or without one. All of the stories handed down in the scriptures show the deep bond the Buddha's own disciples felt for him as their teacher, and that bond continues for serious students on all Buddhist paths today.

—S.R.

24 ॥ *Thirst*

334 The compulsive urges of the thoughtless grow
like a creeper. They jump like a monkey from one
life to another, looking for fruit in the forest.

335 When these urges drive us, sorrow spreads
like wild grass. 336 Conquer these fierce
cravings and sorrow will fall away from your
life like drops of water from a lotus leaf.

337 Therefore I say, dig up craving root and all,
as you would uproot *birana* grass, if you don't
want Mara to crush you as the stream crushes
reeds on its banks. 338 As a tree, though cut down,
recovers and grows if its roots are not destroyed,
suffering will come to you more and more if
these compulsive urges are not extinguished.

³³⁹ Wherever the thirty-six streams flow from the
mind toward pleasure, the currents will sweep
that unfortunate person away. ³⁴⁰ The currents
flow everywhere. Creepers of passion grow
everywhere. Whenever you see one growing
in your mind, uproot it with wisdom.

³⁴¹ All human beings are subject to attachment and
thirst for pleasure. Hankering after these, they are
caught in the cycle of birth and death. ³⁴² Driven
by this thirst, they run about frightened like a
hunted hare, suffering more and more. ³⁴³ Driven
by this thirst, they run about frightened like a
hunted hare. Overcome this thirst and be free.

³⁴⁴ Some, if they manage to come out of one
forest of cravings, are driven into another.
Though free, they run into bondage again.

³⁴⁵ Fetters of wood, rope, or even iron, say the
wise, are not as strong as selfish attachment to
wealth and family. ³⁴⁶ Such fetters drag us down
and are hard to break. Break them by overcoming
selfish desires, and turn from the world of
sensory pleasure without a backward glance.

347 Like a spider caught in its own web is
a person driven by fierce cravings. Break
out of the web, and turn away from the
world of sensory pleasure and sorrow.

348 If you want to reach the other shore of existence,
give up what is before, behind, and in between. Set
your mind free, and go beyond birth and death.

349 If you want to reach the other shore, don't let
doubts, passions, and cravings strengthen your fetters.
350 Meditate deeply, discriminate between the pleasant
and the permanent, and break the fetters of Mara.

351 Those who are free from fear, thirst, and sin
have removed all the thorns from their life. This body
is their last.

352 They are supremely wise who are free from
compulsive urges and attachments, and who
understand what words really stand for. This body
is their last.

353 I have conquered myself and live in purity.
I know all. I have left everything behind,

and live in freedom. Having taught myself,
to whom shall I point as teacher?

354 There is no gift better than the gift of the dharma,
no gift more sweet, no gift more joyful. It puts
an end to cravings and the sorrow they bring.

355 Wealth harms the greedy, but not those who
seek nirvana. Of little understanding, the greedy
harm themselves and those around them.

356 Greed ruins the mind as weeds ruin fields.
Therefore honor those who are free from greed.

357 Lust ruins the mind as weeds ruin fields.
Therefore honor those who are free from lust.

358 Hatred ruins the mind as weeds ruin fields.
Therefore honor those who are free from hatred.

359 Selfish desires ruin the mind as weeds ruin fields.
Therefore honor those who are free from selfish desire.

CHAPTERS TWENTY-FIVE

& TWENTY-SIX

❑ *The Bhikshu & The Brahmin*

THESE CONCLUDING TWO chapters describe what might be called the Buddha's spiritual elite: those who have given up every kind of worldly ambition to dedicate their lives completely to the Eightfold Path. The titles are revealing. Chapter 26 is "The Brahmin," a reference to the highest, priestly caste of the Hindus. Yet the Buddha, as always, judges a person not by external characteristics – birth, status, respectability – but by spiritual growth. "Who is a true brahmin? That one I call a brahmin who has trained the mind to be still and reached the supreme goal of life. . . . It is not matted hair nor birth that makes a brahmin, but truth and the love for all of life with which one's heart is full" (386, 393).

Unlike the brahmin in the Hindu tradition, which he sought to change, the Buddha's brahmin clearly owed nothing to family or heredity; here "caste" is due solely to success in freeing oneself from selfish desire (396). This high estate also shows itself in a patience which is like an army, holding up against blows, verbal abuse, or any other attack (399). A brahmin has crossed the torrential river of craving once and for all. Those who have learned what life has to teach are not compelled by past karma to take on a body again.

These criteria clearly apply to householders – the laity – as readily as to monastics. They are, in principle, within reach of anyone willing to follow the Eightfold Path with complete dedication. Nevertheless, like the founders of the great Christian monastic orders, the Buddha understood that in his time the most suitable environment for working toward such attainments was away from the world, with ties only to others engaged in the same quest. That is why he initiated an order of monks and an order of nuns, whose ideal is the theme of chapter 25.

The Sanskrit name for a Buddhist monk is *bhikshu*, from the root *bhiksh*, "to beg for alms." Bhikshus have no set home and no possessions save robe and begging bowl. They are religious mendicants who go about from village to village, subsisting on the alms obtained from generous householders. A bhikshu does not verbally beg, but simply waits at the door in silence, and is bound to accept whatever is given. This was a prevalent monastic tradition in the Buddha's time, and it is still preserved in Sri Lanka and Southeast Asia.

As with the Buddha's use of the word *brahmin*, however, *bhikshu* here seems to refer less to a member of an established monastic order than to anyone wholeheartedly committed to a life based on spiritual practice. One is a bhikshu, at least in spirit, who accepts with an equable mind whatever life brings, without basing his response on whether what he receives is pleasant or unpleasant (365). Such a person lives not to get but to give. Having set about undoing all set molds of past conditioning, the ideal bhikshu abides in *maitri*, good will toward all life no matter what one's situation (368). The clear application of such verses is not merely to those who wear the saffron-colored robe of a Buddhist monk or nun, but to the spiritual efforts and attainment that are the insignia of anyone dedicated to the path of dharma.

In the Buddha's time, with few exceptions, all who seriously aspired to follow in the Buddha's footsteps became monks and nuns in his orders, including even his father, King Shuddhodana, his wife, Yashodara, and his son, Rahula. That was the way to live as much as possible in the sight and presence of one of the greatest spiritual figures the world has ever seen. Wherever it has flourished, however, monasticism has developed some serious drawbacks, and the Buddhist orders were no exception. In ages much more receptive to the cultivation of the inner life than our own, monks and nuns were generally admired for living an austere life and turning their backs on the pleasures and pursuits that most human beings hold dear. What was not so conducive to spiritual growth, however, was their often harsh treatment of the body. In the attempt to smash self-will and break the hold of sensory cravings, many monks and nuns resorted to strangling the senses and breaking down not only self-will but the spirit of the human being. Such practices are diametrically opposed to the spirit of the Buddha's Middle Path, even though many later monastic followers of the Buddha practiced such methods with zeal.

With verses like 369 – "Bhikshu, empty your boat! It will go faster" – it is easy to understand an ardent young monk or nun wanting to throw out every personal attachment, even at the expense of physical health, to reach the alluring goal of nirvana. In their immense enthusiasm to move in exactly the opposite direction in which their senses were pulling, however, they often forgot that the Buddha also emphasized the importance of keeping the body strong and fit. He rejected asceticism completely. It is incorrect to think of the Buddha as a shaven-headed mendicant who ate only leftovers put in his bowl. In the Indian tradition, alive even today, when such a one as the Buddha arises, villagers happily set aside the best they have to put in his bowl, even if it means their families must do with less. Overzealous followers may have starved and wracked their bodies, just as monks and nuns have done in other religious traditions, but the Buddha himself advocated a long, healthy life in the service of all.

Though addressed to a monastic community over two thousand years ago, the truths in these two chapters are just as valid today, and the joyful states of consciousness are still within reach of everyone. While it is unlikely that the extraordinary affluence of our age will reverse itself in a rush to renounce the world, the voluntary simplicity of the Middle Way is an ideal with growing appeal. In these verses we can see the outline of a life permanently fulfilled on every human level.

−S.R.

25 ॥ *The Bhikshu*

³⁶⁰ Train your eyes and ears; train your nose and
tongue. The senses are good friends when they are
trained. ³⁶¹ Train your body in deeds, train your
tongue in words, train your mind in thoughts.
This training will take you beyond sorrow.

³⁶² He is a true bhikshu who has trained his hands,
feet, and speech to serve others. He meditates
deeply, is at peace with himself, and lives in joy.

³⁶³ He is a true bhikshu who keeps repeating his
mantram, lives simply, and explains the dharma
in sweet words.

³⁶⁴ He is a true bhikshu who follows the dharma,
meditates on the dharma, rejoices in the dharma,
and therefore never falls away from the dharma.

365 He is a bhikshu who is content with what he
receives and is never jealous of others. Those who
are jealous cannot do well in meditation.

366 Even the gods praise the bhikshu who is contented
and lives a pure life of selfless service. 367 Free from the
desire to possess people and things, he does not grieve
over what is not. 368 With friendship toward all and
faith in the Buddha's teachings, he will reach the holy
state where all is peace.

369 Bhikshu, empty your boat! It will go faster. Cast
out greed and hatred and reach nirvana.

370 Overcome the five obstacles, rise above the five
selfish attachments, and you will cross the river of life.

371 Meditate, bhikshu, meditate! Do not run after sense
pleasures. Do not swallow a red-hot iron ball and then
cry, "I am in great pain!"

372 There can be no meditation for those who are not
wise, and no wisdom for those who do not meditate.
Growing in wisdom through meditation, you will
surely be close to nirvana.

³⁷³ When a bhikshu stills his mind, he enters an empty
house; his heart is full of the divine joy of the dharma.
³⁷⁴ Understanding the rise and fall of the elements that
make up the body, he gains the joy of immortality.

³⁷⁵ Learn to be wise, O bhikshu! Train your senses;
be contented. Follow the teachings of the dharma
and keep pure and noble friends. ³⁷⁶ Be a friend
of all. Perform your duties well. Then, with your
joy ever growing, you will put an end to sorrow.

³⁷⁷ As the *varsika* plant sheds its faded flowers, O
bhikshu, shed all greed and hatred. ³⁷⁸ He is a bhikshu
who is calm in thought, word, and deed, and has
turned his back upon the allurements of the world.

³⁷⁹ Raise yourself by your own efforts, O bhikshu; be
your own critic. Thus self-reliant and vigilant, you
will live in joy. ³⁸⁰ Be your own master and protector.
Train your mind as a merchant trains his horse.

³⁸¹ Full of peace and joy is the bhikshu who follows
the dharma and reaches the other shore beyond
the flux of mortal life. ³⁸² Full of light is the young
·bhikshu who follows the dharma. He lights up
the world as the moon lights a cloudless sky.

26 ॥ *The Brahmin*

383 Cross the river bravely; conquer all your
passions. Go beyond the world of fragments
and know the deathless ground of life.

384 Cross the river bravely; conquer all
your passions. Go beyond your likes and
dislikes and all fetters will fall away.

385 Who is a true brahmin? That one I call a
brahmin who has neither likes nor dislikes
and is free from the chains of fear.

386 Who is a true brahmin? That one I call a
brahmin who has trained the mind to be still
and reached the supreme goal of life.

387 The sun shines in the day; the moon shines
in the night. The warrior shines in battle, the

brahmin in meditation. But day and night the
Buddha shines in radiance of love for all.

388 That one I call a brahmin who has shed all
evil. I call that one a recluse whose mind is
serene; a wanderer, whose heart is pure.

389 That one I call a brahmin who is never angry,
never causes harm to others even when harmed
by them.

390 That one I call a brahmin who clings not
to pleasure. Do not cause sorrow to others;
no more sorrow will come to you.

391 That one I call a brahmin who does not
hurt others with unkind acts, words, or
thoughts. Both body and mind obey him.

392 That one I call a brahmin who walks in
the footsteps of the Buddha. Light your
torch from the fire of his sacrifice.

393 It is not matted hair nor birth that makes a
brahmin, but truth and the love for all of life with

which one's heart is full. ³⁹⁴ What use is matted
hair? What use is a deerskin on which to sit for
meditation if your mind still seethes with lust?

³⁹⁵ Saffron robe and outward show do not make
a brahmin, but training of the mind and senses
through practice of meditation. ³⁹⁶ Neither riches
nor high caste makes a brahmin. Free yourself from
selfish desires and you will become a brahmin.

³⁹⁷ The brahmin has thrown off all chains and
trembles not in fear. No selfish bonds can ensnare
such a one, no impure thought pollute the mind.

³⁹⁸ That one I call a brahmin who has cut through
the strap and thong and chain of karma. Such
a one has got up from sleep, fully awake.

³⁹⁹ That one I call a brahmin who fears
neither prison nor death. Such a one has
the power of love no army can defeat.

⁴⁰⁰ That one I call a brahmin who is never angry,
never goes astray from the path, who is pure
and self-controlled. This body is the last.

⁴⁰¹ That one I call a brahmin who clings not to pleasure, no more than water to a lotus leaf or mustard seed to the tip of a needle. ⁴⁰² For such a one no more sorrow will come, no more burden will fall.

⁴⁰³ That one I call a brahmin whose wisdom is profound and whose understanding deep, who by following the right path and avoiding the wrong has reached the highest goal.

⁴⁰⁴ That one I call a brahmin whose wants are few, who is detached from householders and homeless mendicants alike.

⁴⁰⁵ That one I call a brahmin who has put aside weapons and renounced violence toward all creatures. Such a one neither kills nor helps others to kill.

⁴⁰⁶ That one I call a brahmin who is never hostile to those who are hostile toward him, who is detached among those who are selfish and at peace among those at war.

⁴⁰⁷ That one I call a brahmin from whom passion and hatred, arrogance and deceit, have fallen away like mustard seed from the point of a needle.

⁴⁰⁸ That one I call a brahmin who is ever true,
ever kind. ⁴⁰⁹ Such a one never asks what life
can give, only 'What can I give life?'

⁴¹⁰ That one I call a brahmin who has found his
heaven, free from every selfish desire, free from
every impurity. ⁴¹¹ Wanting nothing at all, doubting
nothing at all, master of both body and mind,
such a one has gone beyond time and death.

⁴¹² That one I call a brahmin who has
gone beyond good and evil and is free
from sorrow, passion, and impurity.

⁴¹³ That one I call a brahmin who has risen
above the duality of this world, free from
sorrow and free from sin. Such a one shines
like the full moon with no cloud in the sky.

⁴¹⁴ That one I call a brahmin who has crossed
the river difficult and dangerous to cross,
and safely reached the other shore.

⁴¹⁵ That one I call a brahmin who has turned
his back upon himself. Homeless, such a one
is ever at home; egoless, he is ever full.

CHAPTER TWENTY-SIX

⁴¹⁶ Self-will has left his mind; it will never return.
Sorrow has left his life; it will never return.

⁴¹⁷ That one I call a brahmin who has overcome
the urge to possess even heavenly things
and is free from all selfish attachments.

⁴¹⁸ That one I call a brahmin who is free from
bondage to human beings and to nature alike,
the hero who has conquered the world.

⁴¹⁹ That one I call a brahmin who is free from *I*,
me, and *mine*, who knows the rise and fall of life.
Such a one is awake and will not fall asleep again.

⁴²⁰ That one I call a brahmin whose way no
one can know. Such a one lives free from past
and future, free from decay and death.

⁴²¹ Possessing nothing, desiring nothing for their
own pleasure, their own profit, they have become
a force for good, working for the freedom of all.

⁴²² That one I call a Brahmin who is fearless, heroic,
unshakable, a great sage who has conquered death
and attained life's goal.

⁴²³ Brahmins have reached the end of the way; they have crossed the river of life. All that they had to do is done: they have become one with all life.

▯: Glossary

THIS BRIEF GLOSSARY is a guide only
to Sanskrit and Pali terms in this volume. Words used once
and explained in context are not included. As a rough guide,
Sanskrit and Pali vowels may be pronounced as in Italian or
Spanish. The combinations *th*, *dh*, *ph*, and *bh* are always pronounced as the consonant plus a slight *h* sound: *th* as in *hot-
head* (not as in th*i*ng); *ph* as in *haphazard* (not as in ph*o*ne).

arya [Skt.; Pali *ariya*] Noble, civilized, cultured; in Buddhism,
   holy, a saint.
ashrava [Skt. "flow"; Pali *asava*] The outflow of attention or
   consciousness inherent in a conditioned mental state.
atman [Skt. "self"; Pali *atta*] Self, oneself; in Sanskrit, also a
   technical term for the transcendent Self of the Upanishads.
bhikshu [Skt. "one who seeks alms"; Pali *bhikkhu*] A religious
   mendicant; a fully ordained Buddhist monk.
bodhi [Skt. & Pali "awakening"] Enlightenment; the illumination of consciousness that comes when the mind has been
   stilled.

bodhisattva [Skt. "one whose nature is enlightenment"; Pali
bodhisatta] One who strives to become a Buddha through
many lives; the Buddha before his enlightenment; in
Mahayana, a Buddha who vows to go on being reborn in
order to help others.

Brahma [Skt.] God as Creator (not to be confused with *Brahman*, the transcendent Godhead of the Upanishads).

brahmin [Skt. *brahmana*] Member of the priestly caste.

Buddha [Skt. "awakened"] A title for one who has attained
enlightenment.

deva [Skt.] A god or divine being, superhuman but not the
supreme Deity.

dharma [Skt. from *dhri* "to support"; Pali *dhamma*] Law, duty,
justice, righteousness, virtue; the social or moral order; the
unity of life; the Buddha's teaching or Way; also, in a separate sense, a mental state or moment or unit of thought.

dhyana [Skt. "meditation"; Pali *jhana*] In Buddhism, a stage of
meditation or level of consciousness.

duhkha [Skt. "suffering"; Pali *dukkha*] Suffering in the most
general sense; the human condition.

Four Noble Truths The essential teaching of the Buddha: life is
full of suffering; the cause of that suffering is selfish desire;
selfish desire can be removed; it can be removed by following the Eightfold Path.

Four Sights The four scenes (age, illness, death, and renunciation) that prompted Siddhartha to seek nirvana.

Gautama Siddhartha's clan name.

Indra Foremost of the devas.

Jataka Tales of the Buddha's former lives.

karma [Skt. "something done"; Pali *kamma*] Action; an event,
physical or mental, considered as both cause and effect;
the sum of what one has done, said, and thought. The law

GLOSSARY

of karma states that every event is the result of a previous event and must have consequences of the same nature.

loka [Skt. "world, people"] The world; humanity, people in general; a realm of existence, not necessarily physical.

Mahayana [Skt. "large vehicle"] The later of the two branches of Buddhism, followed in Tibet, Mongolia, China, Japan, Korea, and Vietnam.

mantram [Skt. also *mantra*] A short prayer or spiritual formula.

Mara [Skt. from *mri* "to die"] Death, the Striker or Tempter; embodiment of the selfish attachments and temptations that bind one to the cycle of birth and death.

nirvana [Skt. *nir* "out", *va* "to blow"; Pali *nibbana*] Extinction of selfish desire and selfish conditioning.

samsara [Skt. "that which is in incessant movement"] The cycle of birth and death; the world of change. The only thing that is not samsara is nirvana.

samskara [Skt. "intense doer"; Pali *sankhara*] A deep mental impression produced by past experiences; a mental or behavioral complex; the element of personality that is the agency of karma; a thing considered as an object in consciousness, compounded of mental components. In the Buddha's last words – "all things are transient; strive earnestly" – the word for "thing" is *samskara*.

sangha [Skt. & Pali "gathering"] The order of monks and nuns.

skandhas [Skt. "pile"; Pali *khandha*] The five elements of the body-mind complex.

smriti [Skt. "recollection"; Pali *sati*] Recollection of attention, mindfulness.

sutra [Skt. "thread"; Pali *sutta*] The basic principles of a subject arranged for study; a scriptural discourse said to represent the Buddha's own words.

thera [Pali, from Skt. *sthavira* "elder"] An elder at least ten years past his higher ordination, or whose sanctity has earned general respect.

Theravada The older branch of Buddhist tradition, followed in Sri Lanka, Burma, Cambodia, Laos, and Thailand. Its scriptures are preserved in Pali.

trishna [Skt. "thirst"; Pali *tanha*] The craving for personal or selfish satisfaction.

▫️ *Notes*

INTRODUCTION

References are to page number

8 The word *dhammapada* is Pali and is traditionally derived from dhamma, the dharma, and *pada*, path or way. Some scholars take *pada* to mean "word" or "verse"; *dhammapada* then means "Verses on Dharma."

29 Some versions say the prince was taken to the harvest festival not as a child but between the times of the third and fourth Noble Sights, on an outing meant to distract him from his heavy thoughts. The scriptures rarely agree in such details, and anyone piecing together the Buddha's life is forced to choose among variations at almost every point.

36 Two of the Buddha's forest teachers are known to us by name, Arada (in Pali, Alara) and Udraka. We know nothing of their teachings, but can assume they taught Siddhartha how to meditate.

42 "Are you a god?" etc.: Anguttara Nikaya (II.38). This version follows that of Huston Smith in *The World's Religions*.

43–47 This summary of the Buddha's teachings does not follow the actual Sermon at Sarnath, but draws on various sources to convey the essence of the Four Noble Truths and the Eightfold Path.

43 The word "right" (Sanskrit *samyak*) in the Buddha's eight disciplines means not merely "true" or "correct" but "lined up with, headed in the same direction." The eight steps are aligned with each other and with dharma. Each step supports the others, and all are intended to be practiced together in a harmonious integration of inward and outward activity – a "middle way."

44 *Sankalpa*, translated as "purpose," means also thinking, willing, and desiring. Buddhism does not rule out desire, only selfish desire.

44 Right occupation is more than simply avoiding wrong occupation. To the Buddha, the purpose of work is not merely to make a living, but to undo self-centered behavior and unfavorable karma by working for the good of the whole.

45 Right effort is training the will to operate below the conscious level. The Buddha, an unsurpassed psychologist, specialized in ways of doing this. "These are the four right efforts: an aspirant kindles intense desire, strives, generates motivation, exerts his mind, and does his best to see that unwholesome mental states that have not arisen shall not arise; that unwholesome mental states that have arisen shall be expunged; that wholesome mental states that have not arisen shall arise; and that wholesome mental states that have arisen should be sustained, nurtured, augmented, developed, matured, and brought to fruition. In this way, many of my students have achieved perfection through a new kind of knowledge" (Digha Nikaya III.221).

46 *Smriti*, "recollection" or "attention," is also translated as "mindfulness" when part of the Buddhist technical vocabulary. In certain schools, mindfulness exercises include watching one's thoughts without personal involvement in them. Shantideva, an eighth-century monk, wrote: "This in brief is the mark of complete wisdom: again and again, the capacity to watch the changes taking place in the body and mind."

54–67 These traditional stories are drawn from various sources in addition to scripture, including the Jataka, Ashvaghosha's life of the Buddha, and the commentaries of Buddhaghosha. For the full account of Malunkyaputra's questions, see the Majjhima Nikaya, sutta 63. The story of the Buddha's last days is told in the Digha Nikaya, sutta 16. Many more stories and parables are told of the Buddha; two very readable collections are *The Gospel of Buddha* by Paul Carus (Open Court, 1915) and *Footprints of Gautama the Buddha* by Marie Byles (Theosophical Publishing House, 1967).

74 "No-mind" is a concept from the Chinese Buddhist texts. Both "no-thought" and "no-mind" are accurate translations of the Chinese *wu-hsin*, for *hsin* means "mind" or "thought" without distinction. However, since "no-mind" is the familiar English term, "no-thought" is used here for a preliminary state, a fleeting glimpse of no-mind.

81 The theory of dharmas and the "doctrine of momentariness," *kshanikavada*, are greatly elaborated by the Abhidharmist schools of Buddhist philosophy. These paragraphs do not summarize Buddhist doctrine, but use key ideas to illumine what happens in meditation.

THE DHAMMAPADA
References are to verse number

1–2 These two verses use the Buddhist terms *manas* and *dhamma*, which are difficult to render into English. Here *manas* is roughly "thought, mind," and *dhamma* (from Sanskrit *dharma*) has the special meaning of "mental state, moment or unit of thought or experience." The translation here is an effort to give an effective English rendition that catches the meaning of the Pali: that all experiences are a result of thought, that the mind shapes our lives.

7–8 Mara is a personification of all that binds us to the cycle of birth and death. He is always portrayed as an active opponent of the Buddha, "the Striker" who tries to impede the Buddha's progress towards enlightenment.

9–10 The saffron robe is the traditional garb of the monastic. There is a play on words here between the Pali for "stain" and "saffron robe," which are very similar. Like many other Sanskrit and Pali texts, the Dhammapada shows a skill with puns and word play. Verses of this kind are difficult to translate because it is all but impossible to capture the double meanings and subtleties in English.

15–16 The Buddhist scriptures refer to many "worlds (*lokas*)," many states of being in which one can be reborn. As suffering follows a selfish deed in this life, it also determines a painful result in the next life, while good actions lead to a better future. Hindu and Buddhist scriptures share this underlying belief in the law of karma and a multitude of births in many worlds.

21 A favorite word of the Buddha's – *appamada,* "vigilance, earnestness, enthusiasm" – gives this chapter its title.

27 Meditation is a central teaching of the Buddha. Here the verse says simply to meditate earnestly, with enthusiasm.

30 The Dhammapada at times mentions the Vedic gods, in this case Indra, who became lord of the gods through effort. The devas, the gods of the Hindu pantheon, were part of the culture in which the Buddha lived, but they seem to have been minor figures in his inner life: his constant emphasis is on human will, the ability of each person to shape his or her own destiny. But the devas are still a part of the cultural climate, and also meaningful personifications of natural and supernatural forces.

44 Yama is Death, or the god of death and ruler of the dead in Indian mythology. The Buddha at times seems to look upon these figures, the devas, as personifications of physical and mental forces. The devas are not immortals, because after enjoying long lives in the heavenly worlds, they are eventually reborn. The fully awakened Buddhas go beyond even the realms of the gods, into the immortal state of nirvana.

46 In Hindu mythology it is Kama, the god of eros, who is armed with a bow and arrows tipped with flowers. Anyone hit with such a flower arrow is overcome with passion. Here the image is applied to Mara, the Buddha's antagonist, the figure who obstructs him on the spiritual path.

60 The word used in this verse is *samsara,* literally "the world of change and becoming," which is the cycle of birth and death – that is, the world of impermanence in which we live.

66 In this verse "selfish deeds" is a free translation of the Pali *papa*, sometimes rendered as "sin."

79 "Noble ones" is the translation of the Pali *ariya* (from Sanskrit *arya*, "noble"). The Buddha gives a spiritual meaning to this ancient word, originally a name for the Indo-European peoples who migrated to India in the second millennium B.C.

85 Nirvana is often referred to as "the other shore," and the Buddha as a boatman calling, "Who wants to go across?"

89 The Buddhist scriptures reveal a penchant for numbering, perhaps as an aid to memorization. Here the reference is to "the seven fields of enlightenment," which one commentary glosses as "mindfulness, wisdom, vigor, joy, serenity, concentration, and equanimity."

97 This verse is a type of riddle that can be translated in at least two distinct ways. These word games were not uncommon in Pali and Sanskrit.

98 The word *arahant* (Sanskrit *arhat*, "worthy") is used here for the saints and Buddhas who have reached the end of the way.

129 The Pali (and Sanskrit) word *danda* gives this chapter its title. *Danda* literally means "staff," but also "government, punishment."

131 Literally, "If you strike at others with a staff (*danda*)."

136 "The selfish" here translates *dummedho*. While *dummedho* literally means "of faulty understanding," "selfish" is a helpful translation, for what could be more foolish than selfishness?

142 In the Hindu tradition, a brahmin is a member of the priestly caste. Here the Buddha spiritualizes the term and makes it practical.

144 The word translated here as "meditation" is *samadhi,* a yoga term for an advanced stage of meditation.

146 This verse echoes the famous Fire Sermon of the Buddha, in which he states again and again that "all is burning; the whole world is burning."

149 At times the Buddha uses very strong language to shock his listeners out of complacency. Perhaps the gourds left on the ground after the autumn harvest are meant to remind us of the skull, the image of death.

153–154 According to tradition, these are the words the Buddha uttered upon reaching nirvana. Here he calls the ego-driven personality a house that will never be constructed again. The separate life can never be built for him again.

175 There is another reading: "Swans fly on the path of the sun; those with miraculous powers [*iddhi*] fly in the air." Supernatural powers like levitation are said to be accessible through spiritual disciplines. The Buddha consistently stressed that the spiritual life has nothing to do with such powers, which are obstacles that only extend the power of the ego.

190–192 For an explanation of the Four Noble Truths and the Eightfold Path, see pages 43–46 of the introduction. The sangha is the community of Buddhist faithful. The three traditional refuges are the Buddha, the dharma, and the sangha.

197 The Pali and Sanskrit word *sukha* gives this chapter its title.

Sukha is often translated "ease," but also may mean "delight, happiness, joy." It is always contrasted with Pali *dukkha* (Sanskrit *duhkha*), "lack of ease, pain, unhappiness." The Sanskrit prefix *su* means all things that are good, agreeable, to be sought after, while the prefix *duh* means all that is painful, distasteful, and to be avoided.

202–203 These verses use the earthy term *khandha* (Sanskrit *skandha*), "heap," which is here translated as "separateness." The five khandhas are the five "heaps" of which a separate identity is composed: form, feeling, perception, thought, and consciousness. The fourth skandha is *sankhara* (Sanskrit *samskara*), often translated as "thought" but more particularly a conditioned thought, a deep mental impression produced by past experiences. This translation is an effort to render these verses into nontechnical language.

226 "Selfish passions" are the asavas (Sanskrit *ashrava*), the "flowing out" or dissipation of consciousness into fruitless channels, usually said to be four: sensuality, wrong views, becoming, and ignorance.

230 Brahma is the creator god of the Hindu pantheon, not to be confused with Brahman, the transcendent godhead that is beyond attributes.

235 The "messenger of death" is Yama, the lord of the dead.

238 *Dipa* means "lamp" and also "island," so this important verse has two possible translations. This verse echoes the final instructions of the Buddha to his close disciples: "Be a lamp unto yourselves. Rely on yourselves and on nothing else. Hold fast to the dharma as your lamp."

254–255 Here the Buddha is called the Tathagata, "One who has gone this way," a charming name that may have the connotation, "one who has walked in our shoes and shown us the way."

260 *Thera* is "elder," a respected upholder of the dharma. Theravada, "the doctrine of the elders," is a name of one branch of Buddhism.

264–265 The Buddhist monks shaved their heads. These verses play on a popular explanation that a *samana* or homeless ascetic is one who quiets (*sam*) the mind (*mano*).

266 Sanskrit *bhikshu* (Pali *bhikkhu*) comes from the Sanskrit root meaning "to beg," and thus means a monk or mendicant. This verse states that simply relying on alms for livelihood does not make one a spiritual aspirant. *Bhikshu* is "monk"; there is also a feminine form meaning "nun."

268–269 *Muni* means both "silent" and "a sage." Again, the verse points out that observing a vow of silence alone is not sufficient for being honored as a sage. A muni is one who has taken a vow of silence or, in another interpretation, one whose self-will is silent.

270 This verse contains the ancient word *arya*, "noble." Here the Buddha applies it in a fresh way: it is not "noble" to injure any creature.

283 This verse plays on two meanings of the word *vana*: "forest" and "selfish desire." *Nirvana* in this play on words is *nir-vana*, "without *vana*."

285 *Sugata* – "the one who has gone well, the one who has gone by

a good path" – is an epithet for the Buddha. Here it is translated as "one who knows the way."

294-5 These verses clearly refer to allegorical killings, not of the people mentioned but of obstacles to nirvana. This is a common rhetorical device in Indian spiritual literature. The brilliant commentator Buddhaghosha, for example, says that *trishna* and *asmimana*, selfish craving and self-will, are the "father and mother" in that they create the sense of a separate personality. Samuel Beal, an early translator of the Dhammapada, cites a passage in the Lankavatara Sutra, book 3, in which the Buddha makes a statement similar to these verses and then explains the allegory in the same way.

296 Gautama (Gotama in Pali) is the Buddha.

298 Sangha is the community of the faithful. In both Hindu and Buddhist traditions, *satsang*, "spiritual fellowship," is looked upon as an essential practice.

307 "Those who put on the saffron robe": the monastic followers of the Buddha dyed their clothing with saffron.

322 The horses of Sind, now a province of Pakistan, were highly prized.

324 This verse mentions a particular elephant, Dhanapalaka, by name. The commentaries note that even though this elephant was owned by the King of Kashi and received the best of care, he longed to return to his native forest.

339 "The thirty-six streams" is another example of the Buddhist practice of numbering. Often we come across Buddhist refer-

ences to specific numbers: Four Noble Truths, Eightfold Path. Here, the reference to thirty-six "streams," or forms of craving, is obscure.

344 This verse is again playing on the two meanings of *vana*: "forest" and "craving."

350 A more literal translation would be "reflect on what is not pleasant," but the idea behind it is to counteract the natural tendency of the mind to dwell on the pleasant, in order to achieve detachment.

351 The liberated soul has no need to take on another body and be reborn again.

362–365 *Bhikshu* means "mendicant, monk." There are both masculine and feminine forms of this word in Pali. In our modern context, perhaps it is more helpful to think of these verses as applying to any sincere follower of the Buddha.

383–423 These verses were translated especially for use in meditation, so some complexities in the original have been rendered in a more easily understood and poetic form.

392 This reference is to the sacred fire used in Vedic ritual.

393–394 Matted hair and the deerskin are traditional marks of an ascetic. The Buddha is pointing out that these are merely externals, not the heart of practice.

REFERENCES

Citations in the text refer to the following volumes. Following tradition, references are to volume and page number unless otherwise specified.

The Anguttara Nikaya. R. Morris and E. Hardy, eds. Vols. 1 and 5. London: Pali Text Society, 1885, 1900.

The Digha Nikaya. T. W. Rhys Davids and J. E. Carpenter, eds. Vols. 2 and 3. London: Pali Text Society, 1903, 1911.

The Majjhima Nikaya. V. Treckner, ed. Vol. 1. London: Pali Text Society, 1935.

The Samyutta Nikaya. L. Feer, ed. Vols. 3 and 5. Pali Text Society, London, 1884, 1898.

[Sutta Nipata] *Buddha's Teachings; Being the Sutta-Nipata or Discourse Collection.* R. Chalmers, ed. Harvard Oriental Series, vol. 37. Cambridge: Harvard University Press, 1932.

Udanam. P. Steinthal, ed. London: Pali Text Society, 1885.

Vinaya-pitakam. H. Oldenberg, ed. Vol. 3. London: Williams and Norgate, 1881.

🔲: *Index*

THE CLASSICS OF
INDIAN SPIRITUALITY
Introduced & Translated by
EKNATH EASWARAN

THE BHAGAVAD GITA
THE DHAMMAPADA
THE UPANISHADS

"No one in modern times is more qualified – no, make that 'as qualified' – to translate the epochal Classics of Indian Spirituality than Eknath Easwaran. And the reason is clear. It is impossible to get to the heart of those Classics unless you live them, and he did live them. My admiration of the man and his works is boundless."

– HUSTON SMITH, author of
The World's Religions

THE UPANISHADS

Introduced & Translated by

EKNATH EASWARAN

The Upanishads are among the oldest of the Indian wisdom texts. They are the records of teaching sessions given by illumined sages to their students, who were asking the fundamental questions of life: Who am I? What happens to me after death? The sages' responses take the form of flashes of insight, their direct experience of encounters with transcendent Reality.

Easwaran's reliable and readable translation is consistently the bestseller in its field. It includes an overview of the cultural and historical setting, with chapter introductions, notes, and a Sanskrit glossary. But it is Easwaran's understanding of the discoveries of the Upanishads, and their significance to the modern reader, that makes this edition truly outstanding.

Each Upanishad appeals in different ways to the reader's head and heart. In the end, Easwaran writes, "The Upanishads belong not just to Hinduism. They are India's most precious legacy to humanity, and in that spirit they are offered here."

THE BHAGAVAD GITA

Introduced & Translated by

EKNATH EASWARAN

The Bhagavad Gita, "The Song of the Lord," is the best known of
all the Indian scriptures, and Eknath Easwaran's reliable, readable
version has consistently been the best-selling translation.

Easwaran's introduction places the Gita in its historical setting
and brings out the universality and timelessness of its teachings.
Chapter introductions give clear explanations of key concepts, and
notes and a glossary explain Sanskrit terms.

The Bhagavad Gita opens, dramatically, on the battlefield, as the
warrior Arjuna turns in anguish to his spiritual guide, Sri Krishna,
for answers to the fundamental questions of life.

But, as Easwaran points out, the Gita is not what it seems – it's
not a dialogue between two mythical figures at the dawn of
Indian history. "The battlefield is a perfect backdrop, but the Gita's
subject is the war within, the struggle for self-mastery that every
human being must wage" to live a life that is meaningful, fulfilling,
and worthwhile.